D1040111

Teacher Appraisal: A Nationwide Approach

of related interest

Directors of Education - Facing Reform
Tony Bush, Maurice Kogan and Tony Lenney

**Evaluation as Policymaking: Introducing Evaluation
into a National Decentralised Educational System**
Edited by Marit Granheim, Maurice Kogan and Ulf Lundgren

Dedication

This book is dedicated to the co-ordinators of the teacher appraisal pilot projects in Croydon, Cumbria, Newcastle, Salford, Somerset and Suffolk. The teaching profession owes them a great debt.

Acknowledgements

We are grateful to the Department of Education and Science for permission to reprint as appendices its Summary of the National Steering Group's recommendations contained in School Teacher Appraisal: a national framework *(DES 1989) and its list of issues relating to the NSG report on which comments are requested by the Secretary of State for Education. Linda Darling-Hammond's chapter in this book is based on her article originally published in the University of Chicago's* Elementary School Journal *(vol. 86, no. 4, 1986) and we are grateful for permission to use this material.*

We wish particularly to thank Toni Griffiths for her considerable editorial help and Michael Barber for his comments and criticisms of our views on the complicated institutional and conceptual issues involved in a national framework of teacher appraisal. We are very grateful to Janet Friedlander and Megan MacKay for their valuable assistance in shepherding us through the bibliography and to Sally Littlefair, Rachel Norman and Margaret Pike for typing the manuscript and meeting very tight deadlines.

Teacher Appraisal:
A Nationwide Approach

Edited by Alan Evans and John Tomlinson

Jessica Kingsley Publishers
London

First published in 1989 by
Jessica Kingsley Publishers
118 Pentonville Road
London N1 9JN

British Library Cataloguing in Publication data
Teacher Appraisal : a nationwide approach.
  1. Great Britain. Teachers. Performance. Assessment
  I. Evans, Alan II. Tomlinson, J.R.G. (John Race Godfrey), *1932-*
371.1'44'0941

ISBN 1-85302-509-7

Printed and bound in Great Britain by
Biddles Ltd, Guildford and King's Lynn

Contents

Preface

Once misunderstood, once feared, teacher appraisal is now seen not only as necessary but as the lynch pin of professional development and an issue of central importance to the future progress of the education service. Where teachers once were suspicious, they are now - generally - welcoming; they have come to appreciate the idea of appraisal as a means of developing professional skills and knowledge, as a route to relevant training and as a careful way of dealing constructively with shortcomings. The profession has been reassured to find that appraisal has not been brought forward as a crude measure of standards to be applied irrespective of school circumstances and future development.

That this is so is largely the result of the School Teacher Appraisal Pilot Study which followed the seminal report of the ACAS working group. The National Steering Group (NSG) which oversaw pilot studies in six LEAs presented its final report (DES 1989) in October 1989 and concluded that the studies, which involved the appraisal of 1690 teachers and 190 headteachers, provide, 'a sound basis for the development of appraisal throughout England and Wales'. No Secretary of State for Education could have wished for a better springboard for action: careful study followed by clear recommendations. Having noted that the Government expected to make Regulations in autumn 1989 to establish a national framework for appraisal, the NSG identified the key principles and procedures which the Regulations should prescribe and went on to make recommendations as to the guidance that would be needed in a Circular from the Department of Education and Science. The report detailed and justified the main components of the appraisal process. It advised on the conduct of appraisal at every stage, including the selection of appraisers, the arrangements for handling data collection and for handling disagreements and disputes and how the results of appraisal should be documented. It commented on the time-scale for training and implementation, the resource needs and how the results of appraisal should affect the development of teachers and schools.

The benefits of appraisal were listed in the NSG report. They included greater confidence and improved morale, better professional relations and communication within schools, better planning and delivery of the curriculum, wider participation in and better targetting of in-service training, better career planning and better informed references. Further, and of considerable interest to the Government in its plans for schools, the NSG report stressed that appraisal 'should provide a key means of supporting teachers in the implementation of current initiatives, in particular the National Curriculum.' Her Majesty's Inspectorate (HMI) report on teacher appraisal (DES 1989) emphasised that, 'properly resourced and prepared for appraisal can be an effective element in the management of current educational reform.' It is clear that the elements of teacher appraisal are wholly relevant to the implementation of the Education Reform Act.

That appraisal should have emerged as this powerful educational tool is, therefore, something to be welcomed at a crucial stage of the nation's educational planning. However, neither the NSG report nor the HMI report dodge the question of the resources needed to introduce the right sort of teacher appraisal scheme. Its success will 'depend on the provision of adequate resources', says the NSG; 1800 additional teachers will be needed, says HMI. Given the nature of the changes occurring throughout the education service, can this crucial underpinning of necessary development *not* be afforded? On all grounds - professional development, teacher morale, better management, curriculum development, improved teaching and learning - it is clear that appraisal is an idea whose time has come.

The Secretary of State for Education, John MacGregor, may be in danger of missing the moment. Instead of introducing a national appraisal scheme, he has called for a further period of consultation to end at Easter 1990 and has, significantly, re-opened debates which the National Steering Group believed it had settled long ago. Yet there should be one central reason for implementing teacher appraisal and that is to improve teaching and learning. Most schemes around the world have failed because they lost sight of this central purpose. Appraisal can come to be demanded for appraisal's sake and then loses its ability to contribute to professional growth. The arguments that must be come to terms with, which are inherent in the case for a professional development model of appraisal - arguments against merit pay, for confidentiality and thus against governor involvement - are all given powerful voices in this book.

The chapters of this book should provide the Secretary of State and the education service at large with substantial insight into this conception of teacher appraisal. Many of the authors were involved in the pilot studies and in the long deliberations of the National Steering Group and the processes of appraisal   are therefore all given serious attention. Through all the discussion, however, comes the voice of the individual teacher - and that voice is enthusiastic, keen to try, anxious to be honest, wanting more for the pupil, for the teacher, for the school. If good morale is relevant to good teaching, appraisal must not be long delayed.

Alan Evans and John Tomlinson
25th October 1989

Teacher Appraisal: An Overview

Alan Evans and John Tomlinson

In recent times one might be forgiven for thinking that there is something peculiar about the issue of teacher appraisal. Secretaries of State, with chameleon-like adroitness and within a matter of months, have appeared fundamentally to change Government policy; Her Majesty's Inspectorate has at times demonstrated an unusually uncertain grasp of the professional complexities and ramifications involved; and local education authorities have been wary of yet another central Government initiative while recognising that they may have a powerful influence on this most fundamental of professional reforms. Further, despite its delicate - some would say 'high risk' - aspect for the teachers' associations, appraisal has demonstrated the effectiveness and quality of that long-established working partnership between the LEAs, the DES and the teaching profession encapsulated in the National Steering Group for the Appraisal of School Teachers.

Part of the problem is that initiators of (and commentators upon) appraisal schemes have not identified clearly enough the three essential principles involved: purpose, control of data and reciprocity. Opposition to appraisal is meaningless unless its purpose is clear. Most teachers are opposed to appraisal for purposes of merit pay, dismissal or (direct) promotion but not for purposes of professional development, institutional improvement, an improvement in the quality of teaching and learning and in indirect promotion, such as better informed references. As far as control of the data is concerned, teachers will only support a professional system in which teacher appraisal statements have the same confidential status as personnel files. Such a professional system would demand a commitment by teachers to making appraisal work with concomitant expectations of higher educational standards throughout the school system. This, in turn, means better opportunities for professional management. The school management team must demonstrate flexibility and responsiveness when appraisal statements reveal the need for change, whether in the management style, resources, priorities, curriculum or pastoral approach.

These three principles and their interpretation are at the root of appraisal schemes wherever they operate. The failure of appraisal comes about when most of those involved in a particular scheme have felt that the system was unfair and neither in their own interests, in the interests of their fellow professional workers nor in the interests of their employers.

It is understandable, if sad, that the first direct Governmental move in this complex arena was the confused and illogical paragraph 92 of the White Paper, *Teaching Quality* (DES, 1983):

> 'But employers can manage their teacher force effectively only if they have accurate knowledge of each teacher's performance. The Government believe that for this purpose formal assessment of teachers' performance is necessary and should be based on classroom visiting by the teacher's head or head of department, and an appraisal of pupils' work and of the teacher's contribution to the life of the school. They therefore welcome the interest currently shown amongst employers and teacher associations about career development and professional assessment of teachers.'

This paragraph suggests that the Government and its advisers had learnt little from the disastrous attempts to introduce appraisal in other countries (for example, the United States of America) and from the fact that the weakest schemes were those that made classroom observation their central concern and paid little or no regard to professional development, school improvement, confidentiality of data and the use of the appraisal interview as the central vehicle. Nearer home, substantial sections of British industry in both the private and the public sector were moving away from the forms espoused in paragraph 92.

As far as the appraisal of teachers was concerned, the next two years were largely wasted, with Government spokespersons choosing to emphasise some or all of the main points of paragraph 92 as if the various elements were coherent, obvious, universally applicable and economic in implementation - none of which was the case. The Government White Paper, *Better Schools* (DES, 1985), which contained a number of commendable sections, still remained conceptually and intuitively weak with regard to professional appraisal:

> 'The Government holds to the view expressed in *Teaching Quality* that the regular and formal appraisal of the performance of all teachers is necessary if LEAs are to have reliable, comprehensive and up-to-date information necessary for the systematic and effective provision of professional support and development and the deployment of staff to best advantage ... Taken together, these decisions should result in improved deployment and distribution of the talent within the teaching force, with all teachers being helped to respond to changing demands and to realise their full professional potential by developing their strengths and improving upon their weaknesses; with the most promising and effective being identified for timely promotion; with those encountering pro-

fessional difficulties being promptly identified for appropriate counselling, guidance and support; and where such assistance does not restore
performance to a satisfactory level, with the teachers concerned being
considered for early retirement or dismissal.'

The language had changed. Appraisal had replaced assessment but the conceptual error remained, namely, the idea that appraisal for promotion, dismissal, professional development and career development was a linear list
of mutually dependent purposes commanding trust and confidence. This
major flaw in the thinking of Sir Keith Joseph, then Secretary of State,
brought out the worst in most of the teachers' associations. At a meeting on
the proposed appraisal of teachers held at the DES a month after *Better
Schools* was issued, a leader of one of the major teachers' associations stated
that appraisal chipped away at the bargaining position of teachers and therefore had to be opposed. Teachers' acceptance of it could not be bought simply by providing more money for induction and in-service education. A
representative from one of the headteachers' associations chose not to challenge the key paragraphs of the White Papers cited above but, instead,
raised a number of key issues: first, who was going to assess teachers? second, what criteria would be used? third, what would be the resource implications? Above all, he stated that the salary implications could not be
ducked. Only two of the representatives of the teachers' associations raised
professional issues which suggested that the key paragraphs of the two
White Papers formed a very dubious base from which to embark on such a
major debate.

Paragraphs 182 and 183 of *Better Schools*, however, put down markers
for the establishment of a national framework for appraisal, possibly enshrined in statutory regulations, and the need for an agreement between the
local authorities and the teachers' associations on appropriate local structural and organisational arrangements for a national framework. This development or possible shift in policy was to prove significant in the years
ahead.

The debate on appraisal developed as 1985 wore on. In the summer, HMI
issued *Quality in Schools: Evaluation and Appraisal* (DES 1985) which represented a major step forward in the Inspectorate's thinking: it clearly ruled
out any direct link between appraisal and dismissal.

Sir Keith Joseph, in one of the few moments when spleen overruled in-
tellect, stated: 'I am saying, not that appraisal has to be connected with merit
pay, but that the whole subject should be discussed ... The one inexcusable
thing is to refuse to discuss it, which is what the teachers' unions are doing.'
Yet, as is clear from the foregoing, the teachers' unions were certainly discussing it.

In Birmingham in November, at a national conference of representatives
of LEAs, teachers' associations, higher education, HMI and the DES, Sir

Keith cleverly and sensitively redefined the debate, not just on appraisal, but on assessment, evaluation and monitoring and the role of central government, the local authorities and the teaching profession in providing an effective education service in an advanced, technological society. By doing so, he forced the teachers' associations (and to a lesser extent the LEAs) to examine the full professional implications of appraisal and their role in leading the profession as well as in safeguarding the interests of their members. Sir Keith, at a stroke, had adroitly shed several, but not all, pieces of encumbering accountability baggage and had indicated a willingness to embrace some of the points being raised by those pressing for school improvement if such mutual espousal were to lead to pilot work which would eventually develop into a national scheme in this vital policy area of teacher appraisal. Ironically, his endeavours were to bear fruit in a strange way several months later.

1986 was to prove a disastrous year for the teachers' associations for they were to lose their bargaining rights on salaries and to have imposed upon them national conditions of service. Yet, the Advisory Conciliation and Arbitration Service Working Party on Appraisal, involving representatives of the teachers' associations, the LEAs and the DES, was to produce a seminal Report which enshrined principles and processes on which teacher appraisal in the pilot studies (in Cumbria, Croydon, Newcastle-upon-Tyne, Salford, Somerset and Suffolk) was to be based from 1987 to 1989. The teacher representatives never allowed the agenda to run away: they kept faith with their members but came out of the negotiations with the most cogent and coherent framework for appraisal of the decade. On this aspect of negotiation no party could fear that it had been found wanting. These 'ACAS principles' enshrined the three features of an appraisal system which could be acceptable to most workers, whether professional or blue collar. They were and are a necessary trio in any appraisal scheme which is to lead to genuine improvements in quality but they are not in themselves a sufficient condition for such success. The pilot studies were to give penetrating insights into the challenges of moving from innovation to implementation and institutionalisation and into the need to consider the educational and professional ramifications of these processes at school, local and national level.

The ACAS principles and processes were to serve as a guide for innovation and change. They proved to have a suppleness and flexibility that allowed institutional and individual growth and development while guarding against injury and licence which could be both wasteful and frustrating. As the pilot studies progressed, proposals and arguments based on experience began to emerge which gave a more sophisticated understanding of the need for, and character and scope of, a national framework, of the nature of discretion and flexibility within a local education authority and, within such a framework, of a concept of the latitude which a school might need in establishing an appraisal scheme. The pilot studies have indeed provided a new frame of reference for appraisal as an agency of professional development and institutional change and the educational use to which the outcomes of appraisal can be put. These developments are documented in later chapters by Ray Bolam, Agnes McMahon, Howard Bradley and individuals from several of the pilot authorities. It is an exciting tale, and a remarkable one, given the inauspicious beginnings of the debate on teacher appraisal in this country.

But we rush ahead of our tale: the intellectual roots of appraisal and the appraisal process itself must first be examined. Then, before turning to the experience of appraisal outlined in the following chapters, we speculate on the possible impact of appraisal in the period ahead, the 1990s.

The origins of teacher appraisal

It would be a mistake to attribute the growing interest in teacher appraisal only to the thinking associated with increasing the accountability of schools: it is as much connected with the school improvement movement. Indeed, teacher appraisal, broadly conceived, sits more comfortably within the context of schools being encouraged to review their curricula methodology and to develop better means of assessing pupils' learning and the effectiveness of school processes than within a narrow context of criticism of teachers, talk about the failings of the education service and the search for and castigation of inadequate teachers.

It is important to appreciate that both streams of activity - political criticism of schools and attempts to make schools more effective - have existed side by side, especially since the mid-1970s. Moreover, they have interacted in some interesting ways. The agenda for greater public involvement in education and for more public accountability announced by James Callaghan at Ruskin College in 1976 also released a hitherto suppressed professional agenda among those in the education service who wished to widen curricula and make them more appropriate - especially to achieve 'secondary education for all' - and who welcomed the opportunities of broader alliances in local communities and industry in support of education enterprise.

The trend in the 1960s and early 1970s had been to pay regard to those who suggested that schools had little effect on their pupils. Compared with the influences of race, gender and social background, educational outcomes were mainly non-educationally determined. It required a political programme aimed at making education socially and economically useful, as well as promoting individual autonomy, to help counteract such a climate of opinion. It gave credence to research such as *Fifteen Thousand Hours* (Rutter, 1979) or Prof. Maurice Galton *et al*, in *Inside the Primary Classroom*, (1980), and, more recently, *School Matters* (Mortimore *et al*, 1988). And it was paralleled by curriculum and organisational development in both primary and secondary education which showed how important it was to have 'whole school', collegial approaches to curriculum planning, staff development and organisational development. In this way the concept of the professionalism of teachers has been significantly extended. Schools were on the move from being collections of individual practitioners to being also collectives of practitioners. The self-critical, self-developing school began to appear and its values to be recognised. It became the model for the matrix within which significant change could be attempted optimistically. Formerly, many attempts at change had been blunted on the classroom door.

In secondary education, an important part of this process was the HMI/LEA *Curriculum 11-16* project from 1977-83. In primary schools, the movement towards creating 'curriculum leaders' within a school's staff followed the criticisms of the 1978 HMI Primary Education Survey. The *Curriculum 11-16* project's final Report (DES, 1983) quoted a headteacher, speaking of the whole school approach to curriculum reappraisal: 'I know of no other way in which a complete school can concentrate its attention and concerns on the fundamental reason for its existence ...' (p. 7). For a 'whole school' policy to be effective, two conditions have to be satisfied. There must be effective leadership and 'the other is the ability to provide an appraisal, in the context of the school's overall aims, of particular pieces of work undertaken by departments or groups of teachers and children' (p. 8). Three years earlier it had been possible to report from the experience of one of the participating LEAs: 'The object was to find a means through which a school could undertake curriculum reappraisal in a way that would involve all staff looking at the school's total provision ... Schools were asked to design their own means of appraisal' (Tomlinson, 1980, 19-20). The reports of the enquiries mounted by ILEA, *Improving Secondary Schools* and *Improving Primary Schools*, reinforced the concept of teachers being reflective and self-critical about their individual and collective work. The idea of a school development plan was urged in the primary schools report.

By 1985, as we have seen, the Secretary of State's White Paper was called *Better Schools* and, following the 1986 and 1988 Education Acts, schools have become the focus for all the major strands of policy: they are the means by which parental choice is exercised in the market place; they are the unit of financial managements and accountability; they are the engine for the national curriculum and assessment programmes; and their governing bodies are the vehicle by which the community and business interests express their aspirations and exercise the formal powers conferred upon them.

This, then, is the political and professional context into which the appraisal of teachers will be introduced. It helps to explain the polarity between schemes which concentrate on criticising teachers as individual practitioners and those which acknowledge the context within which teachers carry out their tasks, both individually and collectively, and the spirit of the aspirations and approaches negotiated with the LEA and the local community through the governing body. Are we seeking teacher appraisal, performance review or performance improvement? Is our aim to reinforce the notion of the individual practitioner or is it to acknowledge and contribute to collegial approaches to teaching and 'whole school' improvement?

The appraisal process

Purposes

In the previous section, we analysed the differing and contradictory origins of demands for the introduction of teacher appraisal. The nature and effectiveness of this appraisal depend on recognition of the fact that there is irreconcilable conflict between a scheme based on accountability and one whose purpose is professional development.

In an accountability model, the aim of appraisal is to assess a teacher's performance in order to make decisions about dismissal, promotion or possible merit pay. This is the view that informed Sir Keith Joseph when he first declared the Government's interest in teacher appraisal. It still played a part in Government thinking as late as the *Better Schools* White Paper in 1985. As Sir Keith Joseph put it, 'The regulations might also require local education authorities to take account of the outcome of appraisal in managing their teacher forces and possibly the continued employment as teachers of individuals assessed as unsatisfactory.' It is also a view which has been advocated in some parts of the popular press.

In a professional development model these purposes are rejected entirely. Appraisal becomes not a reward and punishment mechanism but a process which should result in development in both the skills and career prospects of the individual teacher and lead to improvements at school or institutional level. In short, the aim in this model is not control but the improvement of teaching and learning.The two contrasting models are alternatives. They cannot be combined successfully, though many schemes, in particular in the USA, have attempted to do this. The reason is straightforward. The success of the professional development model depends on teachers being open, frank and forthright during the process. They must be able to discuss problems and constraints or engage in constructive criticism of aspects of the management of the school. If it is to bring about individual and institutional improvement, appraisal must therefore be a two-way process which takes place in an atmosphere of trust and confidentiality. However, if appraisal includes elements of the accountability model - merit pay or dismissal, for example - these will clearly deter a teacher from the very openness and frankness which underpins the success of the professional development model. As Linda Darling-Hammond says, accountability based schemes lead inevitably to 'teacher resistance or apathy'.

Since the scheme is to be implemented throughout England and Wales, it is absolutely essential that any confusion about purposes be avoided from the beginning, otherwise massive investment will have been wasted. An accountability model would not only fail to improve teaching and learning, it would involve frittering away hundreds of millions of pounds which might have assisted the funding of other pressing educational innovations, such as those stemming from the educational reforms of the late 1980s.

Scope

The scope of what is being attempted is worth dwelling on briefly. It is intended that appraisal will apply to all of the 400,000 teachers in England and Wales, including, on an equal basis, headteachers. It is likely too that LEA education departments will be obliged - morally at least - to introduce appraisal for their staff. At a time of multiple change, this is a daunting task. Indeed, unless LEAs are able to dovetail appraisal with other changes, so that it assists rather than hinders their implementation, then it will be unworkable.

The scope of the scheme also needs to be examined from the point of view of the individual. What elements of that myriad of daily tasks which make up a teacher's work are to be included in the scheme? The 1986 Education Act, which gave the Secretary of State the power to introduce teacher appraisal, included:

> 'the performance of teachers ... (a) in discharging their duties and (b) in engaging in other activities connected with the establishments at which they are employed ...'

The agreement in ACAS narrowed the focus considerably:

> 'Appraisal should be related to the teacher's job description which will reflect the balance between the teaching load and other duties outside the classroom.'

This emphasis on the job description has been maintained in the pilot studies and the refinement of thinking over the pilot period on the scope of appraisal is a good example of the value of piloting major innovations.

Frequency

The pilot studies have also shed light on the vexed question of how often each teacher should be appraised, though the pilots did not provide a conclusive answer. As is so often the case, the question can be answered better if it is rephrased. The critical educational question is, 'How long should the teacher appraisal cycle be?'

For reasons which are explored in the following chapters, the option of an appraisal cycle of between one and three years has gathered extensive support, since it is seen as minimising the disadvantages of both the one-year and three-year options, while ensuring that appraisal can be a continuous process. Since, however, appraisal needs to dovetail with the INSET process, a two year cycle seems preferable to a four or five term cycle. The importance of the review meeting one year after the main appraisal interview should, however, be emphasised in the process so as to be genuinely 'continuous'.

The choice of appraiser

Knowing who will appraise whom is at least as important to most teachers as knowing when and how often appraisal will take place. The question is also at least as complex.

On one factor, there is universal agreement. No one without proper training should act as an appraiser. The technical and professional demands of appraising a teacher's work - involving, for example, a high level of interviewing and classroom observation skills - are such that *high quality* training is essential. Establishing that, however, does not answer the far larger questions of which groups of staff should be entitled to appraise and to what extent an individual teacher should be able to choose his or her appraiser. Both questions require examination and this is done in the chapters which follow. They show that the pilot studies would appear to lend weight to the case for senior managers, rather than peers, as appraisers.

The question of how much choice of an appraiser should be available to individual teachers is examined by contributors to this book. Complex issues arise concerning free choice, management decision, staff decision and negative preference and great care is needed in the whole process, the most important aspect of which is credibility of the scheme as a whole to those involved.

The appraisal cycle

The details of the appraisal cycle are examined in more depth elsewhere in the book. Generally, the pattern that has emerged is roughly similar across all six authorities. The appraisee and appraiser meet at the beginning of the cycle to discuss the process ahead. This important meeting is followed by a period of information-gathering during which not only classroom observation takes place but also such other written and oral information is sought as has been agreed by both parties.

Classroom observation is the element of the process which does most to arouse suspicion at first. It is interesting that teachers who have completed an appraisal cycle tend to suggest that their fears are unfounded and all those involved report that classroom observation skills do not come naturally and they must therefore feature as a high priority in appraisal training.

One lesson of the pilot studies is the importance of self-evaluation as part of the information gathering. If a teacher is to benefit from appraisal and establish targets for improvement, his or her self-assessment is critical. The pilot studies have shown that this too is demanding for the appraisee. They also reveal that in general teachers are far more willing and able to talk about what they perceive to be their weaknesses than about their strengths.

Once the data are gathered, the appraisal interview, which is the centrepiece of the process, can take place. There has been little controversy about this aspect of the process and the rewards come from discussing aspects of work with a fellow professional in a confidential atmosphere. By the end of the interview the appraiser and appraisee should have agreed targets. The nature of the targets is important too for the credibility of teacher appraisal will depend also on the extent to which these can be met.

The agreed statement and its follow-up complete the appraisal cycle. The following two sections examine two critical and controversial aspects of this part of the cycle.

Reciprocity, professional development and resources

Teacher appraisal is time-consuming, professionally demanding and is being introduced at a time when the teaching profession is managing a tidal wave of change. If, in these circumstances, teachers are prepared to participate in appraisal, they are surely entitled to expect something in return. This is what is meant by reciprocity. It is a necessary condition for the successful implementation of appraisal, for teacher commitment to the scheme will not be forthcoming unless the new obligation brings with it a new entitlement and this necessarily involves resources and in-service training.

The precise effects of appraisal or INSET demand are difficult to predict. Some of the demand resulting from appraisal would have been felt in any case; some ought to have been revealed but for one reason or another could have been suppressed; some of it would coincide with local strategic priorities; some, indeed, might change perspectives on what those priorities should be. The effects of appraisal on demand will therefore vary from area to area according to the sensitivity of the INSET process in the past, turnover of staff and a host of other factors. Two things, however, can be stated with certainty. First, it is likely that appraisal will result in a substantial net increase in demand for professional development opportunities. Any other outcome would fly in the face of experience generally about the effect of consulting people on their needs. Second, however much LEAs and schools have in their INSET budgets when appraisal is implemented - and given the pressure of change in the next five years the amount will never be 'enough' - it is essential that at both local and institutional level there is a sum earmarked for meeting the outcomes of the appraisal process. This will not only ensure that reciprocity is a reality, it will also be an important signal to the profession that the reciprocal nature of appraisal is recognised at the outset.

Confidentiality

If the entitlement to professional development that appraisal implies is one critical element in winning teacher commitment, ensuring confidentiality of appraisal is another. If teachers are to be frank, open and forthcoming in the appraisal process, they must be reassured that the contents of their appraisal discussions will not be reported except in strictly controlled circumstances. It is important to emphasise, therefore, the obligation of confidentiality which this places on every appraiser. Loose talk, to adopt a second world war phrase, could cost a whole school's appraisal scheme. This much is obvious. The much more complex question is what becomes of the formal record of each appraisal known as the appraisal statement. The reports of those involved in the pilot studies confirm that this is perhaps the most sensitive issue for teachers involved in appraisal. The teachers' associations clearly recognised this in all the discussions from ACAS onward.

The position arrived at by the National Steering Group is that appraisal statements are to be viewed similarly to other confidential personnel documents with access strictly limited by rules laid down nationally. Appraisal statements are to be kept in the school, not at LEA offices, and are available only to the appraisee, the appraiser, the head and the CEO or his or her representative. To ensure that the INSET and other developmental needs identified during the appraisal process can be acted upon without widening access, each appraisal is also to produce a 'development note' which lists such identified needs. The content of this must also be agreed by both appraiser and appraisee.

It is clear that, whatever arrangements are made for confidentiality, there will be tensions as the national scheme is introduced. Given that the success of any appraisal scheme depends overwhelmingly on teachers' commitment to it, it is essential that the question of confidentiality is handled extremely sensitively when the scheme is implemented. This will mean ensuring not only that national guidelines are accepted but also that there are no breaches caused by administrative inefficiency. Careful procedures must be established and enforced to ensure that errors are avoided. If headteachers or teachers came to believe that their appraisal statements spent days in an in-tray before being filed, it could undermine confidence in an otherwise excellent scheme.

Institutionalisation

In the next section we shall speculate briefly about the longer-term influence of teacher appraisal. However, it is appropriate to conclude this review of the appraisal process by issuing two notes of caution; one concerns resourcing of appraisal in the future, the other the need for continuing commitment beyond the implementation phase.

There is no need here to examine the detailed discussions on the resourcing of appraisal that have taken place in the National Steering Group. Nevertheless, some general observations can be made. Unless teacher appraisal is given, and is seen to be given, priority in allocations of time and other resources, it will fail. This in turn implies commitment from the top: the CEO and the education committee. Summarising a study of several American school districts, McLaughlin and Pfeifer argue in *Teacher Evaluation* (1988) that 'the willingness of teachers and administrators to take up the problem of teacher evaluation depended on ... the express and strong commitment of the superintendent to teacher evaluation'. Ultimately, it will not be merely the words spoken but the allocation of resources that indicates whether this commitment is genuine. In addition, unless resources are available, then the time in which appraisal takes place will be so strictly limited that it becomes of necessity a perfunctory chore. If this occurs, it will not achieve the ambitious aims established for it and will therefore not be worth even the limited expenditure it has incurred.

Continued commitment is another concern. The pilot studies have generated tremendous enthusiasm among participants. Most of those involved have found it a valuable process. Whether this commitment is maintained in the long term will depend critically on two factors. First, it must be seen to continue to have practical outcomes, whether they be improvements in school organisation or professional development opportunities for individuals. Second, it must become part of the process of educational change and development at school and local level, rather than a bolted on additional activity which does not relate to other processes. In short, appraisal will require the development of an 'evaluation culture' which values activities that question assumptions and traditional practices and seek out alternatives. As one participant in the pilot studies explained to the evaluation team, 'whole school' review, appraisal and INSET all contributed to a 'questioning atmosphere'. McLaughlin's and Pfeifer's conclusions, based on empirical work, support this view. Their developmental perspective leads them to reach 'two broad conclusions for teacher evaluation. One is that it takes time to establish the norms and culture essential to teacher evaluation. A second is that the process of building that culture continues well beyond the first stages of getting started'. In the next section it is to that 'beyond' that we turn.

Appraisal and the future

So far we have explored the origins of teacher appraisal and examined the major debates over the process it involves. Here we shall assess its potential impact on the education system in the decade ahead. Clearly, some of the suggestions that follow are highly speculative and, given the many uncertainties in the short and medium term, there has perhaps never been a less auspicious time for predicting the outcome of a major education reform. Nevertheless, we believe that it is worth attempting, partly because it may help to raise the level of debate, but also because it may assist the process of implementation if those responsible for it have the more distant effects in view. Columbus, after all, reached America steering by the stars.

A warning

It is worth recalling the importance of implementing appraisal sensitively. That is not to suggest it should be done at snail's pace: it is to point out that unless the teaching profession gains confidence in the process - which in today's climate requires adequate funding and consultation at all levels - then appraisal could become an expensive and bureaucratic millstone. As such, it might satisfy those whose only interest is in the appearance of accountability but it would not result in improved teaching or learning. It is also worth bearing in mind that this has been the fate of the majority of teacher appraisal schemes across the world. There is, for example, no evidence that the Hong Kong scheme which gave teachers a mark out of ten on 27 aspects of teacher behaviour including 'co-operation with the school authorities' brought about an improvement in educational provision. The same could be said of a Florida scheme which tried to assess, among other things, 'Teacher Withitness'(*sic*).

Potential benefits

Fortunately, the experience of the six pilot authorities is of a different order because the schemes implemented have scrupulously pursued a professional development model. As a result, the reports from all of them are positive, even enthusiastic, about the potential benefits of the scheme.

Individual teachers have welcomed the opportunities appraisal has afforded them to receive positive feedback on their work. The negotiation of their job description and the targets for the future have provided a sense of purpose. There has been an opportunity to discuss the wider issues of career development and also to make constructive comment on the constraints the school may place on an individual's work. Some teachers indeed have seen it as a chance to 'lobby'. There is little doubt in the pilot authorities that appraisal has improved job satisfaction. It is interesting too that research at Nottingham University has suggested that appraisal can help to reduce levels of stress for teachers. If this view is confirmed it will accord with the research carried out in industry and commerce.

All these benefits clearly assisted the schools as a whole. Appraisal is also a mechanism which enables schools to bring coherence to their development plans, to establish priorities and to offer better targeted INSET. The greater levels of communication between professionals which appraisal generates, the exchange of ideas and the sharing of experience, particularly when prompted by classroom observation, are also beneficial.

The enthusiasm of those involved in the pilot schemes should, however, be tempered. Pilot authorities and the schools and teachers within them were volunteers and hence by self-selection likely to be those most committed to the scheme. The Education Support Grant funding they received was at a level which will not be replicated in the national scheme. Also, participants admit there may have been a 'Hawthorne' effect with perhaps the national focus and local priority given to appraisal, rather than the intrinsic qualities of it, generating some of the benefits.

Even so, if only a fraction of the benefits is diffused by the national scheme across England and Wales, then it will be a major step forward. Our first conclusion would therefore be that, if teacher appraisal is carefully and sensitively introduced, which given the other pressures on schools and LEAs will be a substantial achievement, it will result in a higher quality of professional relationships and ultimately in improved teaching and learning.

As we have continually indicated, the implementation of teacher appraisal coincides with that of other important reforms. We shall now look at the crucial interrelationships between teacher appraisal and these other developments: first, those relating to the monitoring and evaluation of achievement (in its broadest sense) in school, including the national curriculum, assessment and testing, records of achievement and the question of performance indicators. Second, we examine relationships between appraisal and those aspects of reform which relate to the management of the school, including LMS (Local Management of Schools) and the role of governing bodies. Finally, we explore the role of appraisal as an element in the process of change itself.

Appraisal, achievement and evaluation

We have already pointed out that teacher appraisal, as it was conceived before the pilot studies, had its origins in two contending forces: the school improvement movement and the drive since the 1970s for accountability. The ACAS agreement and the recently announced national scheme represent in large part a victory for the former. The pilot studies, for example, placed great value on the process of 'whole school' review, some even claiming that it was an essential element in the appraisal process. By contrast, attempts to relate appraisal directly to assessments of pupil performance were rejected out of hand by the National Steering Group. Elsewhere, however, the accountability forces have made dramatic strides forward, not least in the Education Reform Act with its requirements for the publication of assessment and testing results. As a consequence of these contrasting forces, tensions can be expected as appraisal is introduced.

On the one hand, the institutionalisation of 'whole school' review which appraisal is likely to prompt (where it has not happened already) will bring about greater management coherence in many schools and give them a sense of direction. Moreover, given the relationship such reviews will have to appraisal, they are likely to be based firmly on collaborative management processes with extensive professional participation. This would be a wholly welcome development offering greater professional satisfaction and also, if the 'School Matters' research (Mortimore *et al*, 1988) is correct, the likelihood of improved achievement. Taking it a step further, the whole school review ought surely to inform the budgetary process which schools will be developing under LMS.

On the other hand, the publication of test results will take place. These will be important indicators of a school's success; more important, in public perception they are likely to be given even more weight than they deserve, particularly in the early days of their existence. Parents and governors are bound to ask questions about results which they consider are unsatisfactory. That, after all, is the avowed purpose of the legislation. In some cases it will be possible to trace back sets of results to individual teachers. In these circumstances it can be expected that the integrity of the professional development model outlined in the national scheme will be threatened. If it survives it will provide a mechanism both for supporting teachers who are unfairly under attack on the basis of published results and for discovering routes to improvement for others. If it does not survive, it will go the way of so many other appraisal schemes. Its survival will depend on robust defense and indeed promotion of it by the profession and perhaps most of all by headteachers. The defense will be greatly strengthened if its effectiveness becomes manifest; hence evaluation of the national scheme in its early stages will be important. It will also be strengthened - and this is probably critical - by the openness with which the profession meets other calls for accountability. The idea of a profession accountable to no one but itself is long since dead.

In this respect, the present debate about performance indicators is important. Some such indicators are clearly for internal monitoring purposes but others will be of interest externally. If parents are to make effective use of their increased powers of choice they will require high quality information about schools, otherwise they will base decisions on misinformation or vague notions of reputation. Educational professionals will need to recognise this and ensure that the information they provide about schools gives a full and accurate picture, not one which is based narrowly on, for example, examination results alone. If in this way the teaching profession recognises the legitimate rights of parents to information about the school's performance in the broadest sense, then its case against lay involvement in the essentially professional process of appraisal will be watertight.

Nevertheless, in spite of this separation of powers between the lay person and the professional, the appraisal process will be linked to the indicators of the school's performance. 'Whole school' review will provide the connection, for clearly no review can be carried out without reference to the various publicly-recognised performance indicators to which the school works. Furthermore, such a review will no doubt result in the school establishing targets against those indicators for the future. These will provide an important part of the context for teacher appraisal. Professionals in schools will be able to defend exclusion of governors from the appraisal process on the grounds that only a professional development model can make possible the improvements in teaching and learning required to meet the whole school's established targets. In short, the defense of a professional appraisal process depends on a trade off: if parents and governors demand improvement in the accountability of each tree, they lose the wood.

Appraisal and the locally managed school

However successfully the profession makes this defense of appraisal as a professional process, it is clear that governing bodies will be aware of the appraisal process and some of its consequences. They will be responsible for managing the resource framework within which appraisal targets are met. Finally, they will expect to see the continuing improvement in the quality of provision in the school on which the defense of appraisal for professional development will depend.

Pressure on appraisal for professional development can be expected to vary in intensity according to circumstances. In the past any pressure governing bodies have exerted has mainly been felt, absorbed or transmitted by headteachers. Heads will continue to be the main link between the professional staff and the governors in the future. It has been widely commented on that heads can expect governors to become considerably more active across a much wider range of aspects of the school's work than they have been in the past. This is an inevitable consequence of local management of schools. Many heads will be able to build on already highly constructive working relationships but they are likely to find the workload daunting. In these circumstances, in larger schools at any rate, it is likely that deputy heads and others with senior management roles will play an increasingly active part in relations with the governing body. Moreover, they are likely to relate directly to the governors so that the head will no longer be seen as the direct link. The end result may be that relations (already typical in industry and commerce) will develop whereby a team of full-time directors answers collectively to the board, albeit under the leadership of the managing director.

This has important implications for appraisal. There are likely to be increasing demands for deputy heads to be appraised according to a process more akin to that of headteachers, in which the governors have a more substantial role. Moreover, heads are likely to have to surrender some of their influence to deputies, who in turn will have to take greater responsibility. It will therefore become acceptable for heads to point out in the appraisal process that for certain substantial areas of responsibility others are accountable. There may also be professional pressure from certain quarters to allow deputy heads as well as heads access to appraisal statements. In the meantime, since this is ruled out by the proposed scheme, appraisal and its personnel implications are likely to remain very much the domain of heads, making it more likely that other responsibilities, finance and resources, for example, will be delegated to deputy heads.

If heads and deputies can be expected to bear the major responsibility for accounting to governors, they can also expect that task to be much more difficult in cases where the school is suffering from tightening financial constraints. This is likely to occur in schools either in local authorities which are being forced to cut overall schools' expenditure or where an individual school is proving less successful in the recruitment battle than its rivals. In such circumstances, governors may well wish to reduce the number of teaching staff. Faced with this situation, governors will no doubt wish to take into account a number of factors such as the salary cost of particular teachers, their appropriateness to the curriculum offered by the school and surely also the quality of their work. Heads and deputies will be consulted and required to offer judgements in such cases. If producing an appraisal statement in support of their views is ruled out as it is under the proposed national scheme, heads will nevertheless offer a view and it seems likely that the views expressed will take account of appraisal statements. A similar process is to be expected where governors are not satisfied with a particular aspect or aspects of the curriculum offered by the school.

Equally, teachers whose jobs are threatened, whether by falling expenditure levels or by inquests into their work by governors, can be expected to use appraisal statements, or at least refer to the contents of statements, in their own defense. Teachers who make no reference to appraisal statements may find themselves condemned by implication.

The separation of appraisal as a professional process from the account-ability purposes of the school will therefore never be total. A number of legal cases or industrial tribunals can be expected to test out these murky waters in the years ahead. It may be that with time, and as the manifest professional benefits of appraisal become apparent to teachers, their sensitivities on the issues of confidentiality will be reduced. However, as we have argued, confidentiality will be essential. In the implementation phase, failure to recognise such sensitivities will destroy the value of the scheme altogether.

The earliest and starkest clashes, it can be predicted, are likely in the City Technology Colleges and Grant Maintained Schools. Here the likely institutional cultures can be expected to challenge the professional defense of the proposed appraisal scheme. The industrial/commercial influences may also press for the heavily managerial styles of appraisal that still exist in some of the less advanced parts of the private sector of the industry. At the same time, increasingly the staffs of such schools will be those who have opted to work in such a climate. Given the cost to such schools of running an effective appraisal scheme, it will be interesting to see whether they opt for superficial accountability schemes and, if so, how soon they realise the extent of time and resources that will be wasted if they do. At present, Grant Maintained Schools are to be included in the national appraisal scheme al-though under precisely what conditions remains unclear. This will mean they have less room for manoeuvre than CTCs; on the other hand, their governors will have to take the responsibility which for most schools will be borne by the LEA. Their powers of discretion are therefore likely to be sub-stantially greater.

Appraisal and educational change

It has become commonplace in educational circles to talk of 'initiatives overload'. One of the ironies of the post-Reform Act world is that in spite of the 415 new powers the Secretary of State accrued in the legislation, in practice the success of his reforms depends on 400,000 teachers in class-rooms. More ironic still perhaps is the fact that the reforms themselves, par-ticularly aspects such as cross-curricular study and group moderation, are only feasible because of developments initiated by teachers over the last two decades.

The challenge currently facing the profession is how to deliver the changes required by the Act while ensuring that the quality of provision is maintained and perhaps enhanced. At a time of low morale and growing teacher shortage this will not be easy. The timetable for implementation set out by the Department of Education and Science is more sensitive to pol-itical reality than to the needs of the schools. Nevertheless, it is increasingly accepted that the era the education sector is entering is one where change will in any case become the norm; certainly, many of the changes schools are currently facing result from social transformations - the effects of information technology, for example - rather than from legislation. If this view is accepted, then the central issue for schools is not how to implement any particular change but how to be able to implement and make use of change constantly. This may prove to be extremely difficult for, while the education system in England and Wales has proved itself capable of generating ideas and initiatives successfully, its record on implementation and institutionalisation is much less good. In short, the creativity of some of the system has foundered on the inertia of much of the rest of it.

It may be that appraisal of the sort proposed in the national scheme provides the mechanism which enables schools and local authorities to come to terms with change in the next decade. Certainly, the opportunity it provides to bring about coherence between the aims of the institution and the assorted aims of the individuals within it ought to assist in implementing reforms. At the most basic level, it is likely to ensure that questions are asked about a range of institutional habits which formerly went unquestioned.

If appraisal successfully performs this function, it will be worth the present levels of investment. Its importance, however, may be greater still. There has been widespread concern, especially within professional circles, about the 'de-skilling' of teaching. Since teachers have lost control of the curriculum in particular, such concern is hardly surprising. What the proposed appraisal scheme offers is an opportunity to stand the educational agenda on its head. While reform emanates currently from the top, appraisal offers teachers a systematic opportunity to make demands from below. This will mean that classroom teachers will be able, in a way that has not been possible in the past, to set an agenda for change of their own. In this way appraisal for professional development could substantially augment the professionalism of teachers in the decade ahead. In return, the centre of the system can expect to see its plethora of reforms delivered. If the pitfalls on the road to a genuinely educational system of appraisal are avoided, therefore, it could provide the foundations of a new and creative partnership between Government and the profession.

Chapter 1

Implementing an Appraisal Scheme in LEAs and Schools

Agnes McMahon and Ray Bolam

Introduction: The pilot schemes

It seems likely that teachers in England and Wales are soon to embark on a unique enterprise. At the time of writing, the National Steering Group is about to submit its final report on the outcomes of the pilot appraisal scheme to the Secretary of State. If all goes according to plan this should result in the publication by the DES of Regulations and a Circular, together with a set of practical guidelines to schools. These four documents will come to be the national framework for teacher and headteacher appraisal which will be, almost certainly, unique in that it will have been nationally agreed by the three key partners - teacher unions, employer associations and the Government. The challenge for LEAs and schools will then be to manage the implementation of appraisal schemes which are consistent with this framework and which respect the particular circumstances of each LEA and school.

The genesis of the pilot scheme was the 1986 report of a Working Group of the Advisory, Conciliation and Arbitration Service. This so-called ACAS Report contained an agreed set of principles and procedures for appraisal which became the foundation of the work of the consortium of pilot LEAs, an approach which was itself recommended in the ACAS Report. The six LEAs involved in the consortium were Croydon, Cumbria, Newcastle-upon-Tyne, Salford, Somerset and Suffolk and the project was funded by the DES from January 1987 to July 1988. The six LEAs differ considerably in size and geographical location, from Croydon which is a compact Outer London Borough with a population of 319,700 and 100 primary and 23 secondary schools, to Cumbria which is a very large rural county in the northwest with a population of 474,400 and 318 primary and 44 secondary schools. The appraisal schemes also varied considerably in their scale and emphases; thus, in Croydon 19 schools were involved in the pilot scheme and in Cumbria about 36 schools participated; in Salford, four models of headteacher appraisal were tried out, in Newcastle 'whole school' review was an optional initial stage, whereas in Cumbria and Somerset all schools carried out a review; Suffolk was able to build upon its extensive earlier research work (Suffolk Education Authority, 1985 and 1987). However, certain major features remained common, for example, each LEA has a co-ordination team, set up various awareness raising activities and trained both appraisers and appraisees.

The purposes of this chapter are to consider the practical implications of implementing appraisal schemes in LEAs and schools, including the teacher appraisal process with classroom observation, headteacher appraisal, awareness raising and training for appraisal, management and resource issues. First, however, we shall give brief accounts of the situation before the pilot schemes took place, and of appraisal as an innovation.

Appraisal as a major national innovation

Two teams of consultants were appointed in April 1987 to assist in the project. The Cambridge Institute of Education acted as evaluators. The National Development Centre (NDC) for School Management Training acted as national co-ordinator and a key feature of the NDC's approach was the support programme of eight workshop conferences (see McMahon, 1987) organised for the co-ordinators from the pilot LEAs. Account was taken of earlier work on appraisal. Formal systems for teacher appraisal have been rare in England and Wales, apart from those used for evaluating teachers in initial training and in their first probationary year. Where appraisals have taken place they have usually been conducted not by the headteacher or a member of the school staff but by LEA inspectors or advisers who have tended to use appraisal 'to assess probationary teachers, to advise on promotions and to look into cases of poor performance' (Turner, Nuttall and Clift, 1986). However, interest in appraisal has grown in recent years and there is now a considerable literature about it (Niblett, 1986 and 1988), although this is usually based on experience of appraisal in single schools or more rarely particular LEAs (James and Newman, 1985 +; Bunnell and Stephens 1984; Turner and Clift, 1985 and 1987). Other studies have recommended particular approaches (e.g. Lyons and Stenning, 1986; Day, Whitaker and Wren, 1987). Two major and influential studies by practitioners were produced by Suffolk LEA as part of a DES funded project (Suffolk Education Authority, 1985 and 1987). All these pre-date the introduction of the pilot scheme. As yet little has been published in England and Wales comparable to the rigorous literature reviews (e.g. Darling-Hammond, Wise and Pease, 1983) or the evaluative surveys of practice (e.g. Wise *et al*, 1984a and b). The exceptions to this are the literature review by Bollington and Hopkins, 1987 and reports produced by the national evaluation team for the pilot appraisal schemes (Bradley *et al*, 1988 and 1989) but these studies were based on pilot work when the ideas about appraisal were being developed. There is a considerable body of literature on teacher evaluation (appraisal) in North America (Darling-Hammond, Wise and Pease, 1983) but this work has two main limitations; first, much of it is based on specific approaches adopted in particular school districts (e.g. Stacey, Kuligowski and Holdzkom, 1988; Nelson, Vanwagener and Brook, 1987); second, it is context-bound and the teacher evaluation processes that are discussed are often significantly different from the type of appraisal scheme that is proposed for England and Wales. For example, the close link that it is anticipated will exist between teacher appraisal and in-service provision in the UK scheme is not usually a feature of US schemes where the focus is much less upon appraisal as a tool for professional development.

The underlying theoretical perspective adopted by the NDC was to regard appraisal as a major innovation which had to be managed at three levels - national, LEA and school. The literature on the management of change is extensive (e.g. Fullan, 1982; Bolam, 1984) but for present purposes it is sufficient to note that a successful strategy for change takes due account of the following key factors:

- the characteristics of the innovation itself, and especially the ways in which members of the target group (i.e. heads and teachers) perceive its feasibility and its costs and benefits;

- the characteristics of this target group of heads and teachers, particularly their morale and attitudes, and of the setting within which they work, especially LEA and schools 'climate', and of the other tasks and innovations to be managed simultaneously;

- the characteristics of the agents or managers of change at each level - national, LEA and school - and especially the perceptions held of them and their motives by the heads and teachers;

- the characteristics of the strategies for change adopted by the managers at each of the above levels - national, LEA and school - and especially the extent to which they take account of the distinctive features, needs and resource requirements of the three key stages in the change process - initiation (or getting started), implementation, and institutionalisation (on a routine basis).

It is beyond the scope of this chapter to pursue the implications of this approach in detail. However, several of them are picked up below and, in particular, the characteristics of the innovation itself are considered.

During the pilot schemes, the concept of the appraisal process (the innovation) went through three major modifications: first, at the outset, appraisal was defined in the ACAS Report; second, it was then interpreted, adapted and implemented in the six pilot LEAs and their schools and this experience was codified in various reports to the National Steering Group; third, it was redefined by the National Steering Group in its final Report, as summarised in Figure 1. Components 1-4 were direct outcomes of the pilot scheme experience but component 5 reflected the fact that, for a combination of financial and professional reasons, the NSG decided to recommend a two-year cycle. The fourth stage of modification will take place when the remaining 110 LEAs implement appraisal in all schools over a four-year period. The rest of this chapter deals with the practical implications of that process.

Teacher appraisal

The basic question for LEAs and schools is: what should be the purposes of appraisal? Within the pilot schemes, teacher appraisal was, from the outset, conceived of as a positive developmental process. The principles set out in the ACAS document provided the starting point for pilot work and these clearly stated that appraisal was understood 'not as a series of perfunctory periodic events, but as a continuous and systematic process intended to help individual teachers with their professional development and career planning, and to help ensure that the in-service training and deployment of teachers matches the complementary needs of individual teachers and the schools'. It was 'intended to raise the quality of education in schools by providing teachers with better job satisfaction, more appropriate in-service training and better planned career development based upon more informed decisions'. Implicit in these statements was an unresolved tension between the individual professional development and the managerial purposes of appraisal. However, the experience gained in the pilot LEAs and schools confirmed the soundness of the original purposes and principles and they became a central plank of the national framework. Certainly more experience was gained about how appraisal could promote individual professional development and inform in-service planning arrangements than about how it might inform LEA policies on teacher deployment. Although this latter purpose was recognised and accepted, it was not a prominent feature of the pilot schemes.

Some additional principles that emerged and gained wide support during the pilot phase were that the appraisal process should be:

(i) open and based on the mutual understanding by appraiser and appraisee of the context, purposes, procedures, criteria and outcomes of the total process

(ii) fair and equitable and be seen to be so both in general and by respecting equal opportunities

(iii) an integral part of a school's staff development strategy and not a bolt-on initiative.

One of the first questions about appraisal that teachers raise is 'who will be my appraiser?' This can be a matter of serious concern which LEAs and

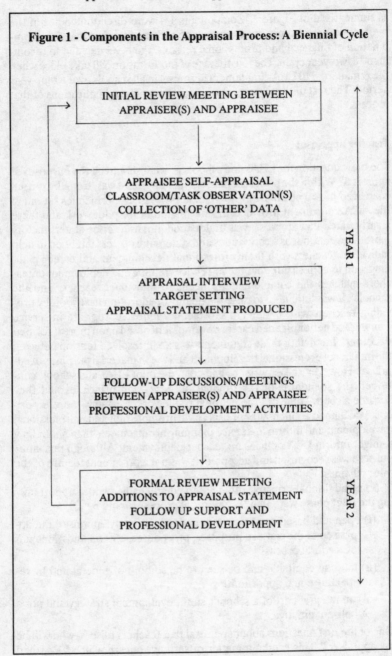

Figure 1 - Components in the Appraisal Process: A Biennial Cycle

INITIAL REVIEW MEETING BETWEEN
APPRAISER(S) AND APPRAISEE

APPRAISEE SELF-APPRAISAL
CLASSROOM/TASK OBSERVATION(S)
COLLECTION OF 'OTHER' DATA

APPRAISAL INTERVIEW
TARGET SETTING
APPRAISAL STATEMENT PRODUCED

FOLLOW-UP DISCUSSIONS/MEETINGS
BETWEEN APPRAISER(S) AND APPRAISEE
PROFESSIONAL DEVELOPMENT ACTIVITIES

FORMAL REVIEW MEETING
ADDITIONS TO APPRAISAL STATEMENT
FOLLOW UP SUPPORT AND
PROFESSIONAL DEVELOPMENT

YEAR 1

YEAR 2

schools will need to deal with carefully. The advice in ACAS was that the appraiser should be 'the immediate superior who may be the head, or other experienced teacher designated by the head'. Initially this was interpreted as a line management approach (e.g. deputy appraises the head of department, who in turn appraises the teachers in the department) but it quickly became apparent that this could not be applied rigidly in secondary or large primary schools, for several reasons. First, there must be a realistic limit on the number of teachers that any one person can appraise given the time that is required; experience shows that an appraiser:appraisee ratio of 1:4 or 1:5 is probably a maximum. Second, many teachers have cross-curricular responsibilities and have no obvious line manager other than the head. Third, there may be circumstances in which the most obvious allocation of appraiser to appraisee would be inappropriate, for instance if it was felt that an appraiser might demonstrate racial prejudice against a potential appraisee. The experience in the pilot LEAs led to the conclusion that the appraiser should be the headteacher or someone specifically designated by the head and that where possible he/she should be someone who had managerial responsibility for the teacher but that this could be interpreted with a degree of flexibility. It was also recognised that the quality of appraisers was crucial. If they are to operate successfully they need to have credibility with their colleagues, a clear understanding of the school's policy goals and INSET resources and the authority to ensure that the appraisals are followed up, with support and resources as required. As a general rule it was recommended that teachers should not choose their appraiser but that they should have the right to ask the head for an alternative if for some reason they felt particularly unhappy about their designated appraiser.

The question about what was the appropriate frequency for appraisal was hotly debated during the pilot project. ACAS had suggested that frequency should vary according to the stage in a teacher's career. Given the timescale of the project, most of the teachers in pilot schools had only one appraisal, although a small minority had two and so received annual appraisal. Experience showed that the logistics of appraising all the teachers in a large school were complex and demanding. Many teachers found the experience of appraisal rewarding but very time consuming - they recognised that the first appraisal had been a learning experience and that the process could probably be conducted more speedily on subsequent occasions but voiced their concern that they might not have the energy to sustain a high quality appraisal every year. In the event the Steering Group concluded that the frequency should be the same for all teachers and headteachers and that a biennial cycle was appropriate. They emphasised that this should not detract from the concept of appraisal as a continuous process and that appraisal should take place and be systematically followed up over a two-year period.

The main components of the appraisal process are set out in Figure 1. There are four main stages: preliminary planning, data collection, the interview and follow-up. These components were suggested in the ACAS document but there was only limited practical advice about what exactly should be done. The experience of appraisal in the pilot schools made possible the more detailed guidance contained in the national framework. Each appraisal cycle starts with a planning meeting between appraiser and appraisee, often called an initial review meeting. This sets out the ground rules for the whole exercise and there is evidence that it can be counter-productive to skimp it. The purposes of the meeting are for both parties to check out their mutual understanding of the process, to agree what data should be collected and to decide on a timetable. The starting point for the discussion is the teacher's job description which should ideally be related to the context of the school's development plan and INSET policy.

On the first occasion this meeting may be quite lengthy, if, for instance, the teacher does not have a clear, negotiated job description. It should be much shorter on subsequent occasions: reference can be made to the last appraisal statement, the targets that were agreed and the extent to which they were achieved. Appraisal is intended to cover all aspects of a teacher's job and though in practice it is impossible to deal with everything in detail, teachers in the pilot schools began by reviewing the whole job before deciding what areas to focus upon. Data collected should reflect the balance of the job description and thus appropriate methods for data collection have to be negotiated. Classroom observation has, from the outset, been regarded as essential but it became apparent that, for some teachers, it may also be appropriate for the appraiser to observe him or her conducting a managerial task (e.g. chairing a departmental meeting) and to consult the head of year about the teacher's contribution as a form tutor. Pilot experience demonstrated the importance of agreeing ground rules for data collection in advance, for instance how classroom observation would be conducted, which teachers might be interviewed, the kind of questions/issues that would be raised and, perhaps most important, what would happen to this raw data.

The pilot scheme experience confirmed the importance of classroom observation in appraisal and, though the majority of teachers had little or no experience of systematic observation and were sometimes very anxious about it, those who did experience it found it very worthwhile. It is important to emphasise that classroom observation in appraisal was not the judgmental process that many teachers experienced as students. Appraisers took great care to negotiate access to classrooms in advance and to discuss with the appraisee how the observation should be conducted. The most widely used style of observation was one based on clinical supervision (Acheson and Gall, 1987). In summary this has involved:

- a short planning meeting between appraiser and appraisee to discuss the content of the lesson and the methods of observation

- observation of the lesson or teaching sequence
- a meeting soon after the observation (e.g. within 48 hours) in which the appraiser and appraisee discuss the lesson and its implications.

The strength of this approach was that it did not put the observer in a judgmental role. The observer's task was to collect evidence about what had happened during the lesson, to share this evidence with the teacher afterwards and then engage in a dialogue with the teacher about the implications of what happened. A note on the outcomes and conclusions formed part of the data considered in the appraisal interview.

Two or three observations were usually conducted as part of an appraisal cycle. Sometimes the first observation adopted a general focus and looked at all aspects of the lesson, while subsequent observations adopted a more specific focus on an important aspect of the teacher's work (e.g. the transition from whole class teaching to group work). Observers sometimes used a standard schedule for the general observation but the conclusion reached at the end of the pilot project was that it would be inappropriate to recommend the use of a standard national checklist of teaching behaviour. The pilot experience highlighted the necessity for criteria on teaching performance to be clarified and agreed in advance by appraiser and appraisee, ideally within the context of department or school policy guidelines. One LEA suggested that all the pilot appraisal schools should agree a teaching policy before starting observations. Criteria will probably always have to be specific to the school or even the department or group but, in future, teachers will no doubt draw upon DES and HMI documents and on publications about the national curriculum. Of course, observation is not the only way of gathering information about a teacher's work in the classroom. Appraisees and appraisers discussed, for example, samples of pupils' work and examination results when this was jointly agreed to be appropriate.

The views of colleagues are potentially valuable sources of data about a teacher's work though naturally the collection of such data has to be handled carefully. A code of practice for data collection was drawn up by the National Steering Group and it emphasises the importance of the appraiser and appraisee agreeing in advance the kind of information to be collected and from whom and also of the appraiser clearly explaining the purpose of the exercise before asking a third party to comment on the appraisee's work.

The third important strand in data collection is appraisee self-appraisal. This was recommended in the ACAS document and an exemplar prompt list was included in the appendix but this component took on greater significance during the pilot work. It became apparent that productive appraisal depended in no small measure on the appraisee's engaging in honest reflection about his or her progress, strengths, weaknesses and developmental needs. Self-appraisal probably has to take place at several stages in the process - before the initial review meeting, before and during data collection and, most important, before the interview. By definition, self-appraisal cannot be compulsory but all the pilot LEAs recommended that it should take place. Some teachers were asked to prepare a written self-appraisal statement, using some agreed headings, and to give this to their appraiser before the interview. Teachers found self-appraisal much more difficult than they had anticipated and, perhaps unsurprisingly, the main problem was that they were too self-critical, rather than self-congratulatory.

The interview is the main component in the appraisal process. It is a discussion between appraisee and appraiser, the main purposes of which are to:

- review the teacher's job description
- review the work done, successes, areas for development identified since previous appraisal
- discuss a plan for development and expectations in certain target areas
- discuss professional development needs
- discuss career development if appropriate
- discuss the points to be included in the final agreed statement.

It was generally agreed that there should be 'no surprises' in the sense that appraisees should not be confronted at the interview with data for which they were not prepared. It rapidly became clear that appraisal interviews were more productive when they were conducted in comfortable surroundings, were uninterrupted, when an agenda for the discussion was agreed in advance and when provision was made for the interview to last for about an hour or longer if necessary. Target setting proved to be difficult as teachers had little experience of it, though it was finally agreed that:

- targets should aim to facilitate the teacher's own professional development
- targets should be agreed in the context of the school's development plan and organisational goals.
- agreed targets should be feasible and realistic in the light of available resources
- some performance indicators which will help to illustrate the extent to which the target is being achieved should be agreed, whenever possible
- targets should be few in number (e.g. 2-5)
- the support that the appraisee will require if he/she is to achieve the targets should be specified and where appropriate the

appraiser should accept responsibility for ensuring that this support is provided

• targets should be reviewed in follow-up meetings and modified as necessary.

Teachers were understandably concerned about what might be written in the appraisal statement and who should have access to it; indeed, this caused more anxiety than practically any other part of the process. The procedure followed in the pilot schools was that towards the end of the interview appraiser and appraisee discussed what should go into the statement, the appraiser prepared a draft version which the appraisee could comment on before it was finalised; then both appraiser and appraisee would usually sign the statement. The appraisee could add a personal note of extension if he/she wished to do so. Great care was taken during the pilot scheme to protect the confidentiality of these statements. The NSG finally concluded that appraisal statements should be treated as very sensitive personnel documents, that a copy should be given to the headteacher and to the appraisee and that it should in principle be available for consultation by the CEO or the CEO's designated representative. In addition, it was agreed that the appraiser and appraisee should prepare a short note detailing the professional development and training targets which could be sent to the appropriate INSET co-ordinator and that the appraisal statement should be the starting point for the formal review meeting in the second year of the appraisal cycle.

The aim for appraisal outlined in the ACAS document was that it should be 'a continuous, systematic process' and implicit in this was the requirement for regular follow up. The main components of the appraisal process (i.e. initial review meeting to the production of the agreed statement) were usually completed within a couple of months, but appraisal is intended to be a continuing professional relationship between appraiser and appraisee, and this has been best sustained through regular meetings. There are two broad categories of follow-up activity: first, the agreed professional development and training; second, appropriate support and encouragement in relation to the continuing agreed targets. Progress can be reviewed relatively informally but it was agreed that in a biennial cycle at least one formal meeting should take place and be recorded on the statement. Sometimes it will become apparent at this meeting that the appraisee's job description has changed and targets will need to be altered accordingly.

Headteacher appraisal

In broad terms, the pilot schemes confirmed that the procedures developed for teacher appraisal could be adapted for headteachers. The components outlined in Figure 1, therefore, apply to headteacher as well as teacher appraisal. Nevertheless, there are some important differences which LEAs will need to take into account. First, there are the basic questions about the purposes and scope of headteacher appraisal. The pilot schemes emphasised the professional development needs of the head but in addition to the purposes that were agreed for teacher appraisal it was generally accepted that appraisal should contribute to improvement in the school's effectiveness. It soon became apparent that it would be impossible to cover all aspects of the head's role in the appraisal and several LEAs developed the practice of selecting about three key areas of work on which to focus. This did raise questions about how and at what stage in the process these areas of focus should be selected. Some concerns were expressed that, when they were identified at the initial review stage when the appraisers were unfamiliar with the school, this might not prove to be as useful as when the selection took place after the appraisers had gained a better understanding of the school context.

A second distinctive feature was that the head's appraisers were external to the school. In the pilot authorities usually two appraisers were appointed, but in some instances only one, and it was concluded that a second appraiser provided a valuable additional perspective. The NSG recommended that both appraisers should be nominated by the CEO and that one should have experience as a head relevant to current conditions in the same phase as the appraisee head. However, the need for LEAs to appoint two external appraisers will understandably make headteacher appraisal more difficult to implement: the appraisers have to be selected, trained and briefed about the schools; at least one and possibly two of them will be unfamiliar with the appraisee's school, so initial preparation and planning may be quite lengthy and could involve more than one meeting; the data collection task is complicated by the fact that appraisers are external, will have to spend additional time travelling to the school and frequently will be unknown to the staff. In contrast, since teacher appraisal is conducted within the school it can be assumed that all appraisers know the context, and the ground rules for data collection can be openly discussed in a staff meeting.

As with teachers, data collection for pilot scheme heads followed the balance of their job descriptions with the main emphasis placed on the agreed areas of focus. It was expected that a headteacher who had a substantial teaching responsibility would be observed in the classroom and the majority of headteachers were observed conducting a managerial task (e.g. reporting to governors, chairing a staff meeting). Interviews with relevant staff and others were a widely used form of data collection but some teachers were uneasy about commenting on aspects of the head's managerial performance because they did not want to appear disloyal.

Unsurprisingly, the issue of access to the headteacher's appraisal statement caused considerable discussion and anxiety. ACAS had recommended that the teacher's appraisal statement should be available to officers authorised by the CEO but said nothing about the head's statement.

However, it was agreed at the end of the pilot work that a copy of the head-teacher's statement should be sent to the CEO. The difficulty was whether or not the governing body should see the statement. The position was complicated by the increased powers given to governors in the 1988 Education Reform Act which included the right to hire and fire staff. It was concluded, however, that appraisal was a professional matter and that the statement should not be shown to the school governing body. However it was recognised that the governors should be informed about the proposals for action arising from the appraisal where these had implications for matters for which the governors were responsible.

Awareness raising and training

The introduction of teacher and headteacher appraisal is a major innovation to the school system, one that is bound to cause considerable anxiety at the outset. The pilot schemes invested heavily in preparation and training and this undoubtedly positively paid off. Experience showed that the introduction of appraisal was facilitated when LEAs took steps to raise awareness about appraisal and build a climate of mutual support and trust. They did this in several ways: for instance, senior officers were explicit about their intentions for appraisal (e.g. how to phase it in, use that would be made of information arising from appraisal), consultative committees which included representatives of teacher associations were established and involved in the design of the local scheme and any accompanying materials, information about appraisal was widely disseminated and consultative meetings were held with headteachers to enable them to raise any concerns they had. In addition, heads were given some discretion about the timetable for introducing appraisal into their schools in so far as this was possible. Similarly, appraisal was introduced more smoothly in schools where the staff respected and trusted each other, where they had access to information about appraisal and where they were given opportunities to discuss the scheme and raise their concerns in staff meetings. A number of schools found that engaging in a school self-review exercise before introducing appraisal (something that was actively encouraged by several LEAs) not only helped to clarify the school's broad policies and goals but also made the teachers more confident about appraisal.

However, awareness raising alone was insufficient preparation; teachers needed training in the specific skills required in appraisal. Appraisee training aimed to clarify understanding of the process and then focused upon classroom observation and interview skills, self-appraisal and target setting. Training for appraisers was more lengthy, usually three or four days as opposed to one or two, and included practice in classroom observation and interviewing, as well as target setting and report writing. Experiential training strategies which gave participants the opportunity to practise particular skills, albeit in simulated settings, and receive feedback on this practice were encouraged. Two key conclusions were, first, that whenever possible the whole staff of a school should receive this awareness raising and preliminary training together so that a common message was received; second, that there should be as short a gap as possible between specific skill training and actual practice of appraisal. Schools intending to phase in appraisal for staff over a given period will need to consider the implications of this.

Managing and resourcing appraisal at LEA and school level

Such a major innovation as appraisal clearly requires specific co-ordination in the early years, though in the longer term it should become an integral part of school and LEA management structures. LEAs have the responsibility of introducing appraisal to the schools, monitoring and evaluating its implementation, overseeing the operation of a complaints procedure, ensuring that the results of appraisal inform LEA management of the teaching force, especially in-service planning, and, finally, organising headteacher appraisal. LEAs were recommended to appoint a co-ordinator, preferably someone with recent school experience at a senior level, to manage these tasks, at least in the initial years. The co-ordinator would, in addition to the tasks mentioned above, maintain contact with schools, organise and possibly help with training, prepare information and training materials and report on the progress of the scheme for local advisory or consultative groups.

Similarly appraisal in school has to be co-ordinated. Sometimes this has been done by the head or by a deputy head with specific staff development responsibilities. Developing a school policy on appraisal in consultation with the staff has been a preliminary task but the co-ordinator has also allocated appraisers to appraisees and checked that teachers understand and are trained for their part in the process. Probably the most demanding task, one that increases in complexity with the size of the school, has been to manage the implementation of appraisal. An appraisal timetable has to be drawn up in consultation with the teachers, requirements for staff cover logged and dealt with, the whole process monitored to check that it is happening as intended, that the necessary paper work is being completed and, finally, the results of appraisal have to be fed into school management discussions, especially the production of the annual INSET plan.

The NSG final report contains detailed proposals on the costing and resourcing of appraisal, and until the Secretary of State has responded to these it is difficult to be specific about the resource implications of appraisal. They are certainly considerable, as was recognised by the National Steering

Group, but it is also clear that in many schools a certain amount of time was already being devoted to what might be termed 'staff personnel management matters'. In summary, the main training costs will be met by LEAs and schools through the LEATGS budget and the use of one or more school closure days. There is provision to ease the implementation of appraisal within the school by providing an element of enhanced staffing to meet the time demands of classroom observation and to provide a reduction in other commitments for appraisers. Nevertheless schools will need to plan carefully how appraisal can be accommodated alongside other tasks. It does bring new demands and there are opportunity costs but the benefits in the longer term should make this worth the investment.

Conclusion: implementing a national scheme

If all has gone according to plan, LEAs will have received a Circular, backed by Regulations, in the autumn of 1989, requiring them to implement an appraisal scheme over a four-year period up to 1993-4 with sufficient extra resources from LEATGS and the Revenue Support Grant. The year 1989-90 is best seen as one of transition and planning. The pilot scheme LEAs will need to consult within their authorities about the implications of the national scheme and then possibly rethink and renegotiate the existing pilot scheme agreements in a national context. Non-pilot LEAs will also need to consult extensively about their own schemes within the framework of the national scheme. In all authorities consultation via the appropriate local consultative machinery will be essential during this transition period. In particular, LEAs will need to ensure appropriate high level LEA officer and adviser involvement in the consultation and negotiation of the scheme. As LEAs restructure their inspectorial and support services, they will also need to take account of appraisal and its requirements. Creating a good atmosphere will be a critical feature of this transition year and LEAs will need to consider ways in which all officers and advisers are and should be appraised as one element in this process. Furthermore, in order to overcome the considerable anxiety and suspicion which still exists, LEA staff should be encouraged to learn from the pilot schemes' experience of the conditions which aid successful implementation. Fundamental to this is a clear vision of the purposes of appraisal, based on the ACAS principles, as a distinctive task which will eventually be integrated into the LEA and schools' continuing work.

The period from 1990-4 is best seen as a phasing-in implementation stage with three main aims:

(i) to put in place an effective and efficient appraisal scheme within the national framework and timetable

(ii) to use available resources wisely and economically

(iii) to protect schools from innovation and INSET overload.

The key decision for LEAs will be how and when to bring schools into the scheme. One option is for LEAs to select schools within the framework of the LEA's development plan and then to provide training on a timetable consistent with this approach, using school closure days as appropriate. A second option is for LEAs to allow schools to select themselves within their own school development plan timetable, to offer a package of training, which schools could choose from according to their own timetable. Such school-led schemes could be approved and monitored by LEAs and this approach would certainly respect schools' discretion and autonomy. Whichever option is adopted, LEAs will need to design their training to be flexible enough to meet school needs and timetables.

It is essential that all LEAs should recognise the need for a central LEA co-ordination role for appropriate consultation and for creating the right climate and for raising awareness. These are essential preconditions if teachers and staff in the authority are to take ownership of appraisal and thus to make it a success. Phasing in is a complex task. LEA co-ordination teams and internal trainers will need both initial and continuing support in order to gain confidence and competence and to ensure that the messages they give are consistent with the LEA's overall scheme and the National Framework. The roles and training needs of both the LEA co-ordination team and internal associate trainers must be addressed in relation to training in awareness-raising and appraisal skills. Lack of resources and time are likely to be major problems, especially if the internal trainers are practising teachers whose first obligation is to their schools.

LEAs and schools will also recognise that appraisal is an aspect of management and staff development. It follows that management training and development should be co-ordinated at LEA level to avoid repetition and duplication, to minimise unnecessary pressure on schools and to make maximum and best use of available resources and people and that appraisal training should be integral to this co-ordinated strategy. If appraisal is to assist in the effective management of change at school and LEA levels it is vital that the right mechanisms and procedures are established. LEAs will be well advised to formulate an overall development plan and to establish a management development training policy based on it. Although the separate activities (e.g. appraisal, TVEI, LMS) may have discrete beginnings, LEAs will ideally think out in advance the sort of structures and procedures that will enable them to be better co-ordinated as people grow in understanding of the common elements of training. To facilitate these processes, LEAs will wish to give serious consideration to establishing a management training steering group and to developing training packages which include core and generic and satellite modules on specific skills, including appraisal.

One final point is worth emphasising: the pilot LEAs were convinced that the benefits of appraisal made all their efforts worthwhile. These benefits include: better planning for professional development, including INSET; better feedback for teachers and headteachers about their work and objectives; a better framework for relating individual staff contributions to the implementation requirements of the 1988 Education Reform Act; and hence, enhanced effectiveness of the school staff as a whole.

Chapter 2

Ensuring Quality in Teacher Appraisal

Howard Bradley

The scope of the national evaluation of teacher appraisal

There will be few people who would dispute the need to evaluate such a huge task as the introduction into schools of the appraisal of teaching staff. How to evaluate it is, however, a very complicated problem.

In the case of the national pilot study for teacher appraisal, the scheme had emerged from a political debate about teachers' conditions of service and remuneration. Different perceptions existed of the purposes of appraisal and there were widely differing views about where one might look to demonstrate the efficacy of such a scheme. Some wanted to look for an improvement in children's learning, others felt one could expect a change in teacher performance or behaviour. Yet others, observing the educational ferment then and still taking place in schools and all the other influences being experienced there, felt it would be difficult to associate any observed change uniquely with teacher appraisal. It certainly was not possible to run a controlled experiment, excluding all other change from certain schools while the effects of appraisal were evaluated, much though some school staff would have welcomed such a respite.

There were also foreseeable difficulties of methodology in the national evaluation. For example, the most obvious method of achieving first-hand information about the central act of the appraisal process, the appraisal interview, would be to observe it. Such was the general view of the delicacy of this event that the idea of a third person observing the other two carrying out this task was universally unacceptable and other means had to be found of exploring how effectively it had been done. There were similar difficulties with another central focus of the pilot schemes, classroom observation.

These problems led the evaluation team from the Cambridge Institute of Education to two decisions. The first concerned the criteria to be used in the evaluation. The team did not set up its own model of appraisal against which to judge the data. Instead, it attempted to represent the views of the various participants as accurately as possible, to analyse that data without loss of meaning and then to interpret it in the light of criteria already established in the 1986 ACAS Report, the LEA appraisal documentation and the literature.

The second decision concerned the methods to be used. We determined to use as broad a base as possible, collecting evidence in all the ways open to us. Our aim was then to devise a method of handling the data which would allow us to combine evidence from different sources and different evaluators so as to produce justifiable generalisations. The method also demanded that we should be able to cross-check any generalisation against all the available data from whatever source. In addition, we hoped to be able to extract parts of the original data to enable us to illustrate the generalisations with examples which breathed reality and enabled the reader to feel empathy with what was happening.

The methods available for collecting information

We collected data in a number of different ways. The principal method was the interview, during which we talked individually to appraisers and appraisees, co-ordinators and headteachers to explore their experience of appraisal and their feelings about it. In some cases we followed individuals through the process so that we could construct a case study of that individual. We also did this with some schools. We augmented the data from interviews by inviting some individuals to keep diaries in which they expressed their day-by-day feelings and concerns about appraisal as well as their activities.

The interview and case study data were supplemented by survey questionnaires which allowed us to establish data about a much larger group of teachers. This gave us information about attitudes before and after appraisal and enabled us to check whether our smaller, interviewed sample was typical of the larger group in the pilot study. We also made use of observation, particularly during training sessions for appraisers and appraisees and in planning and co-ordinating meetings of all kinds.

Our survey questionnaires were conventional examples of the genre. Our observation of training also followed well-trodden paths. It is perhaps more useful to explore here how we established the guidelines for our interviews. As each major aspect of appraisal became clear, one member of the evaluation team took responsibility for determining what kind of data was to be collected about it. Draft proposals were 'shredded' by the whole team and refined to the point where the team member responsible for that aspect produced an *aide-mèmoire* for each of us to use when interviewing. A typical *aide-mèmoire* is that on the appraisal interview shown on page 46. Ultimately, when we were each thoroughly familiar with all the *aides-mèmoire*, we produced two simple schedules, one for teacher appraisal and one for headteacher appraisal, which allowed us to cover the content of each of the *aides-mèmoire*. The teacher appraisal schedule is shown on page 47.

Figure 2:1 - Aide-memoire for data collection
on appraisal interview and follow-up

Please collect information about as many of the following as are possible and appropriate.

1. *Organisation*

(i) who does it to whom?
(ii) a single event or more complex?
(iii) when in the school year? Was there time for data collection, follow-up?
(iv) when will it be repeated?
(v) does appraisal appear to be integrated with other school activities?

2. *Preparation*

(i) what preparation was done on each side?
(ii) what types of data were used?

3. *The interview*

(i) setting and tone? - helping, telling, avoiding?
(ii) time for different aspects of the teacher's work?
(iii) conclusions drawn, targets, etc.?
(iv) what sort of record?
(v) access/use of record?
(vi) views of appraiser/appraisee afterwards about the process? (including emotions)

4. *Follow-up action*

(i) how much?
(ii) how matched into next year's plans, e.g. for INSET, timetable ...?
(iii) who was responsible for ensuring future action?

PLEASE LOOK OUT FOR THE POSSIBILITY OF

(a) audio recording an interview, then later playing it back to both participants separately - what were you trying to do there? etc.

or (b) interviewing before and after, plus audiotaped interview.

Figure 2:2 - Interview schedule for use with teachers after appraisal

Reminders:

1. Please clarify whether your interviewee was an appraiser or appraisee. If they were both, ask questions from both points of view.

2. The following general questions are linked to the seven topics chosen for our reports. They are followed by prompts based on the relevant *aides-memoire*, to enable detailed follow-up in the interview, should time permit.

Questions

1. *How did you feel about the appraisal process?*
   - what do you feel you gained?
   - were there any drawbacks?
   - what changes, if any, would you want in the process next time round?

2. *Can you tell me how the following went?*
   (A) *Preparation - initial review discussion* - length, agenda
     - *self-appraisal*
     - how done/scope/support for/time taken/shared
     - *other preparation*
     - collection of second opinion/scope and time taken
   (B) *Classroom Observation*
     - amount/emphasis/position in cycle/techniques used/who does
        it/nature of preparation and feeback criteria
   (C) *Appraisal Interview/Target Setting*
     - organisation of interview - who involved, when, how long?
     - preparation - what data were used?
     - interview structure - agenda, agreed statement (nature/access/use)
     - type of targets set
     - follow-up action to monitor/enable targets

3. *Looking back, how well do you feel the training you had prepared you for appraisal?*
   - how far did training prepare you for each stage of the process?
   - balance of awareness-raising/information giving and skills development
   - mode of training/trainers/activities/time and timing

4. *What impact has appraisal had (a) on you, (b) on your school?*
   - Look for data relating to change in induction of new teachers/changes in
      ways teachers participate in INSET/new or modified roles/career
      development/help with performance difficulties/use of appraisal
      information in references

5. *How has the appraisal process been organised?*
   - Rolling programme? length of process
   - hours taken? co-ordination of process?

6. *What use, if any, has been made of supply cover?*

7. *What links, if any, have there been between whole-school review and appraisal?*

8. *Is there anything else you want to tell us?*

Figure 2:3 - What sort of things would I put in the diary?

One major purpose of the diaries is to gain a reasonably accurate recording of the sequence of the more formal parts of the appraisal process, e.g. self-appraisal, observation, feedback discussion, appraisal interviews - when they happen, where they happen, how they are conducted. A diary entry of this kind might read:

May 22
Head came in today to do first observation for appraisal. She mingled with the children and the activities which was much better than sitting with pad and pen at back of room like she did with Jim (colleague). We agreed not to set a date together as I wanted it to be more natural than Jim felt his had been.

What sort of entries? - 2

A second purpose is to gain insight into people's feelings and thoughts about these events, e.g.

May 24
Felt the feedback discussion went very well today. Shared some early thoughts on successes as well as concerns. Head v. sympathetic to discipline worries and noise levels. Said she'd noticed it stemming from Winston, Vicky and co. when she observed. Suggested that I might try the 'silent waiting' technique and see what happens. We talked it through at length. Didn't have enough time to discuss other things properly but I feel better for getting the discipline thing out into the open. Felt she wasn't judging me but wanted to help. Felt more relaxed about her than I used to. Arranged second observ. visit before final appraisal interview.

What sort of entries? - 3

A third purpose is to capture any events, with accompanying thoughts and feelings that are not a part of the formal process, but are related to it, e.g. staffroom chit-chat, bits of reading, in-service contact, informal conversations with colleagues, friends, spouse. Again, we are as interested in your thoughts and feelings about these as much as the fact that they happen.

June 4
Chatted to John from Willow Comp. yesterday over coffee before the science study group started at the teachers' centre. He's just had his appraisal interview and we swopped experiences. Made me realise that I haven't prepared myself as well as I might for my appraisal interview. He'd collected a file of notes of his work and

some of the children's work to explain to the deputy (his appraiser), how some of his plans had succeeded and where he was less happy. Thought this was a good technique. Think I'll give it a try if I can find the time. He said he sorts out something for the file about once a week or fortnight.

What sort of entries? - 4

The fourth purpose is to try to understand any outcomes from appraisal, e.g., how, if at all, the experience of appraisal links into people's thoughts and feelings about classroom practice or school developments, or whether it leads to any changes in classroom or school practice. Such a diary entry might be:

July 1
Thinking briefly about next year's PE plans, shall take Mrs Booth's (head) suggestion from app. interview that I look at staff policy document more closely. We agreed that more thought could be given to continuity, so shall talk to Ruth (PE specialist) for advice when I've drafted a plan.

or

July 9
Still thinking about approaches to discipline as discussed with Mrs Booth at appraisal interview. Persisted today with 'silent waiting' technique. Seemed to wait for eternity but it eventually worked. Think the children are beginning to understand. I certainly feel better (and calmer) and noise levels seem to be going down. Will try to catch Mrs Booth if poss. for 5 mins. to talk a bit more about it.

The diaries provided a quite different opportunity to gain understanding of the appraisee's or appraiser's experience. All the diary writers were interviewed by one of the team but we still felt it necessary to establish a common understanding with them and we produced a short booklet covering:

- Why am I being asked to keep a diary?
- What sorts of thing would I put in the diary? This section was illustrated by examples (see pages 48-49).
- Do I have to keep to the style outlined above?
- How often should I make diary entries?
- Can I use another form of recording?
- Who will see my diary?
- What will happen to my diary at the end of the pilot study?
- How useful will my contribution be?
- Will I need to discuss my diary with the evaluation team?

Handling the data

The raw data in the national evaluation consisted of several thousands of items in a number of different formats:

- Individual interview reports - LEA co-ordinators, appraisers, appraisees,
- Observation notes,
- LEA documents,
- Questionnaire returns,
- Diaries.

Each of these documents was held in coded and dated files so that we always had access to the original data.

The raw data from interviews, observations and documents were summarised by the team member concerned at the end of each visit so as to present a report of that particular visit. The summary was done in a matrix form which allows a word processor to match each part of the summary with others according to the appraisal issue or the LEA. The structured questions in the questionnaire were analysed by computer to produce a similar summary. Unstructured questions in the questionnaire were reduced by team members in the same way as other data.

At the end of each term a report has been presented, LEA by LEA and issue by issue. At this stage the team member responsible for each issue (or LEA) receives all the summary data from every evaluator concerning that issue or LEA. Reports on issues or LEAs are then written which are based on data which:

(i) emerged from several sources,

(ii) have been cross-checked with other data and sources,

(iii) have been collected by more than one evaluator.

In a revised form this system for data reduction could be used to facilitate LEA monitoring and evaluation of their schemes, which would have the same multiplicity of sources of data, sites (in this case schools, not LEAs) and issues. LEAs will presumably need similar kinds of regular report, both about school performance of teacher appraisal and about the issues which are emerging across the LEA.

Evaluating the impact of appraisal

Increasingly, as the national pilot study developed, the emphasis of the evaluation changed from reporting the progress of individual LEAs to addressing the major issues which are central to appraisal. Fortunately, there was a starting point in the principles agreed within the ACAS working group (ACAS, 1986). On the nature and purpose of teacher appraisal, the group proposed that appraisal should be regarded as a continuous process, not a series of perfunctory events, and that its purpose should be 'to help individual teachers with their professional development and career planning, and to help ensure that the in-service training and deployment of teachers matches the complementary needs of individual teachers and the schools'.

In particular, the group drew attention to the following six purposes for appraisal:

(i) Planning the induction of entry grade teachers and assessing their fitness to transfer to the main professional grade.

(ii) Planning the participation of individual teachers in in-service training.

(iii) Helping individual teachers, their headteachers and their employers to see when a new or modified assignment would help the professional development of individual teachers and improve their career prospects.

(iv) Identifying the potential of teachers for career development, with an eye to their being helped by appropriate in-service training.

(v) Recognition of teachers experiencing performance difficulty, the purpose being to provide help through appropriate guidance, counselling and training. Disciplinary procedures would remain quite separate but might need to draw on relevant information from the appraisal records.

(vi) Staff appointment procedures. The relevant elements of appraisal should be available better to inform those charged with the responsibility for providing references.

In the event, the entry grade was not introduced, so the first purpose has been approached from the point of view of the new teacher. The six form a set of desired outcomes for appraisal and allow us to develop a series of questions with which to evaluate the impact of appraisal (CIE, 1986):

(i) In what ways has appraisal improved the quality of induction of new teachers? Has it made assessing their performance easier and more reliable? How does it relate to the existing probationer system?

(ii) Has appraisal changed the way in which teachers participate in INSET?

(iii) Has appraisal led directly to new or modified roles for teachers and how have those involved perceived the process?

(iv) Has appraisal successfully identified potential for career development? Has the related support been made available?

(v) Has appraisal helped those teachers who are experiencing performance difficulties? What relationship with disciplinary procedures has emerged? How is this difficult area perceived by those involved?

(vi) What relationship, if any, has emerged between records of appraisal and appointment procedures and references?

Positive answers to these questions would indicate that a teacher appraisal scheme had achieved what it set out to do. More realistically, the answers give us some indication of how far the scheme has improved the situation and in whose view.

In our evaluation work we have been able to collect evidence of positive answers to some of these questions. For the individual we have found it useful to separate 'process outcomes' - those outcomes which have emerged as a result of the individual having taken part in the process - and 'product outcomes' - those outcomes which result from the process having taken place. Among the process outcomes have been:

- greater incentive to reflect
- time to discuss one's work
- the expression of appreciation and recognition
- the growth of confidence and motivation
- a clearer understanding of what is expected, feeling part of the school
- the development of clearer thinking.

Product outcomes for the individual have included:

- skills development, through INSET, experiments with teaching style, often assisted by organisational change
- career development, through INSET, arranged change of role and for the schools:
- improved relationships
- increased knowledge of the school and individuals
- clarification of aims
- productive links between appraisal and school development planning.

Evaluating the effectiveness of models of appraisal

A second aspect of evaluation should help us to improve our understanding of the appraisal process. By examining the means rather than the ends and asking why some things succeed and others do not, we can try to establish what are the influential factors for success. By comparing one model with another we can try to demonstrate how they can be improved.

During the two years of the evaluation of the pilot schemes we have found it useful to organise our thinking into the following categories:

- establishing a good atmosphere and managing the introduction of appraisal
- training
- preparation for the individual appraisal, including data gathering
- classroom observation
- the appraisal interview and target-setting
- follow-up to appraisal.

In addition, we have explored the same group of categories separately for headteacher appraisal because the models adopted differed considerably from those for teacher appraisal, even though the guiding principles were the same.

Establishing a good atmosphere

Both at LEA and school level, preparing the ground has proved vitally important. A number of strategies for doing this have been found successful in our evaluations:

- involving people in the design of the scheme
- encouraging schools to experiment with 'dummy run' trials
- setting up a 'whole school' review as a preliminary to appraisal

- wide-ranging and well-produced awareness-raising activities.

The quality of communication is another important factor to emerge in our evaluations. Well-designed, clear but brief explanatory brochures have contributed to good communication. The work of the LEA co-ordinators has played a crucial role in transmitting a positive message about appraisal and in allaying doubts and anxieties.

Other areas worthy of study are the roles of the co-ordinators in supporting the schools, the roles of LEA officers, advisers and inspectors; the phasing of the introduction and the management of the appropriate time-scales and of supply cover.

Training

The ACAS document said that all teachers should be trained for their part in the appraisal process, appraisees as well as appraisers. We found a degree of consensus among pilot authorities about the length of training for appraisers but that for appraisees showed considerably more divergence. Some had only a couple of hours while others shared the whole of the appraiser training. The evidence suggests that rather more is necessary than the shortest examples quoted. Self-appraisal emerged as a vital component of the appraisal process and one for which training is necessary.

In evaluating training it is also necessary to separate, where possible, awareness-raising activities from training activities. In our view, the two are separate and address different goals. While the distinction is often clear in appraiser training, it is not necessarily so for appraisees. Another area which merits evaluation is the balance between initial training for appraisal and later, complementary training. The trend has been increasingly to regard training as a continuum rather than a one-shot preparation for appraisal.

In examining the content of training, we have noted that some aspects of the appraisal process, for example the interview and classroom observation, have commanded a considerable proportion of the total time available. Other aspects, such as other forms of data collecting, self-appraisal, target-setting and follow-up, have received much less.

We have pin-pointed the high level of skills required of appraisers and we sought some way of categorising the training for these skills to aid generalisation. We found it useful to adopt the categories described by Joyce and Showers (1980). Simplified greatly, they suggest that one can:

(i) lecture and demonstrate skills to people in the hope that they will replicate them

(ii) give them the chance to practise skills in the hope that they will recognise their deficiencies and repair them, or

(iii) give them repeated practice and coaching directed towards improving the skill.

It was reported to us that many skills require training at the most complex level of coaching yet this was most difficult to achieve in practice. This lack of coaching in significant skills could be an influential factor where things do not go as well as expected.

Preparation and data gathering

In all the pilot authorities, substantial supportive documentation has been provided for particular aspects of preparation and data gathering. There is considerable evidence that the quality of shared understanding which evolves as a result of thorough preparation and data gathering can greatly enhance the sense of purpose and the effectiveness of the appraisal.

In many cases, high quality understanding and purposefulness can be traced to the initial review discussion which has taken on an importance which was probably not anticipated in the early stages. Well used, this is the time when the *foci* of the appraisal are agreed, which in effect form the agenda of the appraisal interview. Where it was also agreed that those *foci* needed certain kinds of data to be collected, this has prevented a mismatch between data and discussion at a later stage.

The difficulty of conducting self-appraisal has been mentioned already, yet the importance of self-appraisal is generally recognised. For some, it is the most significant part of the process. For others, it has been a radically new experience for which they felt ill-equipped. Many over-emphasised their weaknesses, often to the exclusion of their strengths. Some were concerned about how frank and honest they should be, worried that their heart-searching might be misunderstood or abused by their appraiser. The trusting and confidential nature of appraisal is crucial here.

Not as much use has been made of the collection of further informed opinion as we had expected, given that the ACAS document went far beyond classroom performances in its list of areas for appraisal. It suggested:

- the teacher in the classroom
- the teacher in the school and the community
- the teacher as manager
- the teacher in the future.

For many of these, other informed opinion would appear to be very useful. It is, however, seen as problematic by many because of a lack of the ethical 'ground rules' necessary to ensure that what is conveyed is more than gossip and hearsay.

Classroom observation

Of all the aspects of the appraisal process, classroom observation appears to have created the most anxiety initially, though this usually disappears in the light of experience.

The concerns for the evaluator centre around the criteria which are adopted, the judgments which are reached and the observation methodology which links the other two. Problems can occur in any one of these three components and we have found wide variation in practice and in skill between one appraiser and another. Training seems often to have identified what not to do or what appraisers are not good at, rather than developing their skills. A wide variety of approaches is employed from the sharply focused to the general 'drinking in the atmosphere', from the participant observer to the 'fly on the wall' approach, from the structured observation schedule to notes made as the events dictated. For some teachers the observations took place over a very short period, for others they were spread throughout a year. Nevertheless, despite the wealth of potential problems, classroom observation was for many teachers a very useful exercise, prompting both appraisers and appraisees to reflect more systematically on their teaching.

The appraisal interview and target setting

The success of the appraisal interview is often determined elsewhere in the appraisal process. The purposeful link between initial review and data gathering bears fruit here in the interview. Where this is the case the agenda for the interview is usually clear. In other cases, the agenda has as its starting point either the self-appraisal, the job description, the classroom observation notes or an interview preparation form provided by the authority.

All the LEAs paid great heed to the need for adequate conditions of privacy and comfort in which to conduct the appraisal. Preparation for carrying out the interview was a central part of the training for appraisers. We received many favourable comments on the conduct of the interviews. The factors isolated by teachers as likely to lead to successful experiences were:

- preparation by both parties involved
- a clear agenda, known in advance
- sharing of documentary evidence
- adequate time
- good interpersonal and interviewing skills
- no interruptions
- giving it a high priority.

Conversely, factors leading to dissatisfaction included:

- inadequate time
- low priority
- sudden changes in the planned programme
- lack of preparation by either or both parties
- not keeping to the agenda.

There seems to have been little difficulty in agreeing the agreed statement after the interview, though some appraisers report considerable difficulty in writing it. The question of who has access to the records may have a significant bearing on the eventual impact of appraisal, as support action for the teacher may depend on the needs established at the interview being made known to various third parties.

The types of target vary. There are those connected with:

(i) classroom strategies, e.g. to make changes in the organisation of the classroom, grouping pupils in a different way or developing a particular teaching strategy such as the introduction of a greater amount of computer-based work

(ii) school performance, e.g. to carry out an additional responsibility such as taking charge of a cross-curricular initiative or taking on a co-ordination role

(iii) career development, e.g. to take on greater management responsibility within the school, or to go on a management course with a view to the next career move.

Most participants produce both long and short-term targets. A number have reported a difficulty in setting clear and specific targets. The participants have, on the whole, kept to six or fewer targets, with a mix of long and short-term, personal and professional.

Follow-up to appraisal

If appraisal is to be part of professional development, some action must take place as a result. Many appraisees have benefited from being able more precisely to identify points for action by them as part of their development. There is also evidence that appraisal has led to more precise identification of INSET needs and to a more exact targeting of INSET provision. It has encouraged the school to use its own capacity to provide professional development as well as to encourage the teacher to make better use of externally-provided INSET. Disappointments emerge where delays occur in handling the agreed statements and more frequently when support for appraisal targets is not available.

Teachers on the whole have not seen appraisal as primarily concerned with career development, though we have some examples of targets which were 'new or modified assignments' which have led already to a career development even in the short time-span of the pilot study. There is a need to explore the issue of confidentiality of documents carefully in this context, for there seems to be a tension between the goal of career development and the principle of confidentiality.

Schools tell us they have gained from appraisal through the development of greater coherence, by the harmonising of individual and school aims. It has also improved communication and increased the possibility of sharing ideas and concerns. There appear to us to be still further gains to be made for the school if the potential usefulness of appraisal as an aid towards school development is exploited. Towards the end of the pilot study we began to find evidence of schools creating systematic ways of using information from appraisals in such a way as to inform the school's policy for staff development, and this is a major step forward.

Monitoring the process in schools and LEAs

Inevitably, the national evaluation has concerned itself with whether teacher appraisal can accomplish the goals prescribed for it by the ACAS Working Group and with comparing the models in the six LEAs to see how each contributes to our knowledge of good practice.

At LEA and school levels there are still evaluation questions to be answered which are similar to those above. There is, however, another set of questions which concern monitoring the process in a school or LEA:

- Is the process being carried out according to the scheme?
- Are appraisers operating consistently and to similar criteria?
- Is somebody checking to ensure that targets are followed up and supported?
- Is it somebody's role to identify cases where things go wrong?
- Can the system handle these unfortunate cases?

In the pilot study, much of the evaluation and monitoring has been for the purpose of developing the LEA's scheme. Increasingly, beyond the pilot study, the monitoring process will need to address questions such as those above. As more schools become involved, the chance of sustained personal contact will decrease and the importance of having mechanisms for monitoring increase. In the pilot LEAs a number of mechanisms have already been tried:

- regular monitoring of appraisal statements and targets by headteachers
- debriefing meetings with each cohort, so that they can influence the scheme for succeeding cohorts

- keeping a log in schools of time and resource demands
- an appraisal book or diary in which school co-ordinators and others write comments
- visits by co-ordinators
- use of a local evaluator
- use of school representatives to feed information to evaluator or co-ordinator.

As teacher appraisal is extended beyond the pilot LEAs to reach all LEAs and all schools, they will need:

(i) to evaluate the introduction of their schemes - preparing the ground, awareness-raising, training and management of the innovation,

(ii) to evaluate the appropriateness of the scheme itself - preparation and data gathering, interview and target-setting, follow-up,

and, in addition:

(iii) to monitor how well the scheme is being applied by individuals and how it deals with any problems which are identified.

The experience of the national evaluation offers some insights into the main components of each of these areas, and the scheme of evaluation adopted for the national study provides a possible structure which might be adapted to suit the needs of LEAs and the scale of their operations.

Chapter 3

Teacher Appraisal and Collaborative Professionalisation

Eric Hoyle

The purpose of this chapter is to explore some of the implications of appraisal for teaching as a profession. In particular, it will be concerned with the implications of the two competing forms of appraisal - *managerial* and *participative* - for the professionalisation, or de-professionalisation, of teaching and its status. Since questions have been raised as to whether the term *profession* retains any meaning and since the attributes which the professions ascribe to themselves are being politically challenged, it is perhaps necessary to begin with a consideration of the concept.

The concept of profession

For most of this century a particular idea of a profession has prevailed. This can be briefly summarised as follows: a profession is an occupation which is founded upon a systematic body of knowledge and the practice of which occurs in circumstances where autonomy is essential if practitioners are to make the necessary judgements in the interests of clients free from bureaucratic or political interference, though subject to the control of a body of professional peers committed to upholding an ethic in which client interests are paramount.

Until recently, this view has been the dominant sociological perspective on the professions and has also been inherent in the rhetoric and strategies deployed by leaders of the professions as they have sought to maintain or improve the status, salaries and autonomy of their members. However, it is now a somewhat discredited view. It has been pointed out (Rueschemeyer, 1983) that it is a perspective limited largely to Britain and the United States and does not account for the relationship between the professions and the state which prevails in much of Europe. It has been shown (Larson, 1977) that the emergence of the major professions has been the outcome of a historical process whereby the exercise of collective power in asserting control over a market for services rather than the provision of a disinterested service of high quality guaranteed by professional self-governance has been the major factor.

Studies of professional practice (Jackson, 1968; Freidson, 1970) have indicated that the knowledge which is utilised is less the systematic body of theory which is central to the traditional concept of a profession than knowledge which is based more on experience, intuition, recipe and common sense. The notion of autonomy has also been determined by many students of the professions (Halmos, 1973) who have argued that the rhetoric of autonomy serves to insulate the practitioner against the need to be accountable to immediate clients or to the public generally (see Hoyle, 1980, for a discussion of these issues).

Thus the traditional concept of a profession has taken a considerable battering in recent years. This has raised the question of whether the concept *profession* retains any validity whatsoever other than as a rhetorical term. One of the leading students of the professions has suggested that the term be dropped and that sociologists should simply study *occupations* without attempting to distinguish a special group termed professions (Friedson, 1983). However, *profession* is an everyday term in constant use and cannot be wholly abandoned by sociologists. Friedson's fall-back position is to urge that wherever the term profession is used its precise connotation should be indicated.

Some of the notions which are central to the traditional concept of a profession are also under attack politically. The radical left has long been critical of the professions as bastions of privilege: 'a conspiracy against the laity' in G. B. Shaw's terms. They are now particularly under attack from the radical right which is challenging their claim to exclusive knowledge, their autonomy and their domination of policy in the areas of law, medicine, education and so forth. The accountability movement which began in the mid-1970s and which was focussed mainly on education has now become a central political issue in relation to all the professions. The major devices for challenging the protectionism attributed to the professions have been to open them up to market forces and, particularly in the case of education, to strengthen the institutions of control at school and national levels.

In the light of the criticisms of the term *profession* one must take seriously Freidson's challenge. The present writer's position is that *profession* as a concept retains considerable *heuristic* value. Although the traditional model of a profession is unacceptable as a description of a particular kind of occupation, it nevertheless draws our attention to substantive issues and their policy implications. We can neither live with nor without the term. If it did not exist, we would have to invent it in order to conceptualise a number of important issues. However, the present writer also believes *profession* is more than simply a heuristic device. In spite of the obvious self-interest which is implicit in the strategic and rhetorical use of the term, it is the present writer's view that it continues to have substance. As Marshall (1963) pointed out, profession is not wholly the invention of selfish minds. There remains a strong ethic of client interest in many professions although they cannot be taken for granted. Nor is it exclusive to occupations commonly called professions, although it might be said to be most commonly found in these occupations. Moreover, it connotes, through the adjective *professional*, commitment, conscientiousness, efficiency, reliability, expertise and so forth. Again, these qualities are not exclusive to the professions and the term *professional* has become only loosely related to its noun of origin though this does not dispose of the fact that it is in the professions where one would expect to find these qualities most obviously displayed.

Much of the current debate about appraisal is being conducted from technical, managerial or political perspectives. This is quite proper. However, although the distinction between political and sociological perspectives is somewhat blurred, it is perhaps worthwhile considering appraisal in terms of the sociology of the professions since it touches on many of the concerns - knowledge, status, control, autonomy - with which it has been traditionally concerned.

Appraisal and professionalisation

Professionalisation connotes the process whereby an occupation acquires over time the characteristics which have been traditionally attributed to the professions. This process entails the creation of a strong boundary sustained by a legally-supported licence to practice, an accredited form of higher education and training, the establishment of a self-governing body, the guarantee of practitioner autonomy, etc. On this definition teaching has been in a process of professionalisation throughout this century, though still falling short of meeting some of the key criteria, e.g. the creation of a self-governing body (at least in England and Wales). The reverse process is, of course, termed *deprofessionalisation* whereby an occupation ceases to meet the criteria either at all or to a lesser degree. The central question, then, is whether teacher appraisal constitutes a further stage in the professionalisation of teaching or is it to be regarded as constituting de-professionalisation. However, before considering this question one must take another look at the term *professionalisation*. Implicit in the concept are two components which are not always distinguished. One entails meeting the criteria of a profession, some of which were given above. The other component is the improvement of the service offered to clients. The two elements might be expected to proceed *pari passu*: control over entry, longer training, increased autonomy might be expected to be accompanied by an increase in *professionality*: the skill, knowledge, responsibility, commitment, etc. of practitioners. However, it is not axiomatic that the two will proceed together and should be kept at least analytically separate. In this section, *professionalisation* is considered largely in terms of increased *professionality*. The final section dealing with status will be more concerned with the other component of professionalisation.

The degree to which appraisal can be said to enhance or inhibit the professionalisation of teachers depends upon the pattern of appraisal which is adopted. Walsh (1987) holds that teacher appraisal can vary according to three dimensions: *focus* (teacher or larger unit), *purpose* (development or judgement) and *form* (hierarchical or collegial). He argues that these patterns cluster to yield two basic forms of appraisal: 'managerial, control-oriented appraisal, which is individually-focused, judgmental and hierarchical; and participative appraisal, which is collectively-focused, developmental and co-operative.' Using Walsh's distinction one can hypothesise that *managerial* appraisal potentially entails deprofessionalisation whilst *participative* appraisal contains the potential for the further professionalisation of teachers.

Managerial appraisal as defined by Walsh would *prima facie* appear to be inimical to the professionalisation of teachers. The judgement of individual competence may not in itself constitute deprofessionalisation. It could be argued that such an approach is *more* professional than the prevailing mode of implicit appraisal which, as Grace (1978) has shown, tends to focus on highly diffuse factors such as personality, good relationships and administrative competence rather than teaching skill.

However, the hierarchical forms of appraisal would appear to be rather more of a barrier to professionalisation. One of the major criteria of a profession is practitioner autonomy and there is substantial literature on the conflict between the principles of bureaucracy and professionality (see Hughes, 1980, for a discussion of the issue). However, the traditional model of a profession has been largely derived from the notion of the individual practitioner. It fails to take adequate account of the fact that the majority of professionals work in organisations of some sort with their inevitable constraints on autonomy. But, as we shall see below, participative appraisal also constitutes a constraint on autonomy. Thus a hierarchical pattern of appraisal can be regarded as leading to deprofessionalisation when combined with the other elements of the managerial approach, particularly when it is underpinned by a limited view of the teacher's role.

Although there is no logical inevitability that such would be the case, it is highly likely that managerial appraisal would focus on a narrow range of teaching skills, perhaps as narrow as those for which pupils' test scores might be taken as proxy. Although it is doubtful whether managerial appraisal would in practice prove to be quite as limited as this, it would most probably take a much more constricted view of the teacher's professional role to that to which we have hitherto been accustomed in this country. Indeed, expectations of the teacher's role have in recent years been expanding to the point of overload (Hoyle, 1988). Many of the forms which this expansion has taken, particularly in the areas of pastoral care, social education, the combating of racism and sexism, etc., are not readily amenable to a narrow form of management appraisal and, insofar as this approach functions to limit the scope of the teacher's role, it might be regarded as inhibiting professionalisation, if not actually leading to deprofessionalisation.

One writes that managerial appraisal *might* inhibit professionalisation because to assert that it *would* do so would be to take a parochial view of teaching as a profession. The British conception of the professional responsibilities of the teacher is much wider than is the case in, say, France (Broadfoot and Osborn, 1988). There the role is seen as much more individualistic and orientated to a more limited set of mainly academic goals. Given that, as pointed out earlier, *profession* is a relative concept, it would be inappropriate to say that teachers in France are 'more' or 'less' professional than British teachers. The argument here is that managerial appraisal is potentially deprofessionalising given current conceptions of the role of the British teacher. It would be conducive to professionalisation only if the professional role of the British teacher was conceptualised more narrowly. It is perhaps ironic that some of those who advocate managerial appraisal are also advocating that teachers should assume wider responsibilities.

Participative appraisal appears to be more conducive to professionalisation on each of the three dimensions identified by Walsh. As its purpose is developmental it is congruent with the concept of professionalisation adopted in this section which is virtually co-terminous with the notion of *professional development* - the continuous acquisition of the knowledge and skills which enhance professional practice. Participative appraisal is congruent with professionalisation because it is collegial in that appraisal is undertaken by professional peers in a spirit of mutual support. Collegial authority is frequently contrasted with hierarchical authority and is held to be the form of authority most appropriate to the control of professional work. Of course, few institutions are wholly collegial and certainly schools remain strongly hierarchical. Paradoxically, however, the introduction of collegial modes of appraisal may do much to offset the constraints of hierarchy.

The relationship between the collective locus of participative appraisal and enhanced professionalisation requires a little more elaboration since it cannot be taken as axiomatic. The assumption of a positive relationship is predicated on the view that effective professional development occurs in the context of the needs of particular schools. This is not to deny the importance of professional development as a process of acquiring academic awards to enhance career opportunities. However, it does emphasise the importance of teachers acquiring the skills and knowledge relevant to the problems of particular schools or, more generally, the educational system as a whole, as innovations emerge and require implementation. Participative appraisal of teachers in terms of their contribution to the development of the school as a whole can be seen as congruent with professionalisation. It constitutes an element in a strategy of school improvement which has emerged in recent years in which professional, organisational, managerial and curriculum development are school-focussed and mutually reinforcing. However, such a perspective on professionalisation would appear to run counter to one of the key elements in the traditional model: that of practitioner autonomy.

Appraisal and autonomy

The autonomy of the practitioner is one of the main criteria of a profession according to the traditional model. Autonomy is never, of course, total even in, say, general medical practice. It is always limited by legal, administrative and financial constraints. And those professionals who work in organisations must yield some of their autonomy in the interests of co-ordination. This autonomy is jealously protected by professional bodies and the teacher associations in particular have fought to sustain the autonomy of members (see Manzer, 1970, for a discussion of some examples). The rhetoric asserts the need for the practitioner to have the autonomy necessary to make professional judgments but, as noted above, critics of the professions argue that this is simply a device for insulating members from the need for accountability.

It is difficult to demonstrate how much or how little autonomy professionals enjoy. However, although comparisons are difficult, it can be suggested that British teachers have enjoyed a relatively high degree of classroom autonomy in terms of curriculum and pedagogy. This autonomy has been eroded in recent years as a matter of government policy and appraisal can be seen as part of this process. *Both* forms of appraisal - managerial and participative - constitute limitations on teacher autonomy. It could be argued that participative appraisal - and indeed the whole of the collaborative approach to professionalisation referred to above - could be seen as a greater threat to autonomy than the managerial form since the intrusiveness of the latter is likely to be limited by the fact that schools are characterised by a structural looseness allowing heads and teachers to collude in the ritualisation of appraisal, observing the form but not the substance. Thus to argue that participative appraisal is conducive to professionalisation entails proposing an alternative to the traditional model of a profession with its emphasis on autonomy.

Such a change in concept appears to be occurring. The pilot schemes for teacher appraisal have been developing a participative mode which is likely to be endorsed as the model to be adopted nationally. This has the support of the teacher associations which thereby appear to be yielding somewhat on the principle of autonomy which they have long defended. A cynical view of this support would hold that the teacher associations, in conforming to the new realism, have accepted the inevitability of appraisal but fought for the participative version as less insidious than the managerial version which they stand ready to oppose should there be any attempt to revert to a managerial version. There may be some truth in this view of the response of the teacher associations but to be set against this view is the fact that for a number of years the teacher associations, to different degrees, have supported the notion of what might be termed *collaborative professionalisation* whereby teachers develop their professionality interactively, learning from each other in a process of curriculum, organisational and professional development, involving such activities as the formulation of development plans, institutional self-evaluation, participation in school-focussed INSET, etc. (see Bolam, 1988; Hopkins, 1986; McMahon, 1986; Holly and Southworth, 1989, for discussions of these developments). This could be seen as part of a process of reconceptualizing the notion of a profession.

However, there remains the problem of the widespread acceptance of *collaborative professionalisation* in general, and participative appraisal in particular, by the profession as a whole. The problem is rendered more acute by the fact that such a development will inevitably be associated by teachers with the many pressures and changes which have been imposed on them in recent years by central government and considerable resistance will need to be overcome. Teachers derive much of their job satisfaction from their classroom autonomy and one cannot be too sanguine about the effective implementation of even participative appraisal. It will need resources, a supportive government attitude to the profession, effective leadership by the associations and, importantly, the prior development of the necessary perspectives and skills amongst headteachers (Bolam, 1986). It will also, incidentally, need a supporting body of research, not least in the area of job satisfaction, building on the work of Nias (1989).

Appraisal and status

In this final section we can return to the more familiar component of professionalisation - the progressive meeting of traditional criteria and the enhancement thereby of occupational status. The question is whether either or both forms of appraisal would enhance the status of the teaching profession.

It may appear unlikely that managerial appraisal would enhance the status of teaching since, insofar as it entails the closer managerial control of teachers, it reduces them to employee status and therefore has the effect of deprofessionalisation. However, a counter argument is that the present status of teachers is depressed because the diffuse criteria of appraisal which apply are such that it is difficult to identify weak teachers and expel them from the profession. Since the public 'knows' that there are many weak teachers, the standing of the profession could, so the argument runs, be enhanced if appraisal facilitated the dismissal of incompetent teachers. It is difficult to assess whether managerial appraisal would have this positive effect on status, though one would hypothesise that such would not be the case. Wholesale dismissals of teachers on the grounds of incompetence are unlikely. There are few wholly incompetent teachers entering the profession (DES, 1988) and thus even with vigorous modes of managerial appraisal, one might expect - particularly in times of teacher shortage - so few teachers to be dismissed that public awareness would not be sufficiently raised to affect their view of the profession. Moreover, insofar as they are aware of such dismissals it may well cause them to have reservations about the competence of those remaining.

Perhaps a more significant issue for status turns on whether or not managerial appraisal serves to limit the scope of the teacher's role and lead to a more explicit emphasis on narrow criteria. This just could have implications for status if, as is often alleged to be the case, the status of the teacher in France and Germany is higher than it is in Britain. However, this would entail a fundamental change in the role of the British teacher and it is unlikely that this would be brought about through managerial appraisal.

Participative appraisal, as part of the process of collaborative professionalisation, might, if the argument advanced in this chapter is valid, lead to enhanced professionality and thus be thought to be conducive to enhanced status. However, this is unlikely. Professional status has deep historical roots and is determined by factors other than professionality, including the diffuse nature of educational goals, the fact that teachers' immediate clientele are young and are in a compulsory client relationship with the inherent problem of control, the large size of the profession and its comparative salary levels, and the fact that everyone has had direct experience of schooling which consequently bears no mystery for them are all factors which impinge upon status. Collaborative professionalisation is undramatic and is, therefore, unlikely to impinge greatly on the general public nor influence the views of politicians, civil servants or academics. It is thus unlikely that it will lead to an immediate improvement of status. It may, however, do so to a limited extent in the long term as general conceptions of the professions change and professionality rather than the factors noted above become more salient. However, in the foreseeable future it is much more likely that we will have a situation of professionalisation without status (Hoyle, 1982), an improvement in the quality of the service without status benefit to teaching as a profession.

Chapter 4

The Appraisal of Headteachers

Victor L. Gane

> *'It sure as hell would lose credibility if the principals and superintendents weren't evaluated!'*

This remark by an American teacher was made to the Suffolk LEA research team during their fact finding mission in North America before the publication of their research (Suffolk Education Authority, 1985). It is a *cri de coeur* which, with the substitution of 'headteachers, LEA officers and advisers' for their American counterparts, would have been heard in most staffrooms in England and Wales when, in 1986, the then Secretary of State proposed legislation to introduce appraisal for the teaching force. In North America, appraisal, or 'evaluation' to give it its North American equivalent, was introduced by most states through legislation during the early 1970s. However, neither the model of headteacher appraisal nor the process could be easily transferred across the Atlantic. For a start there was no single federal model or process, as each state had devised its own scheme with a great disparity in practice and criteria for evaluating what was good teaching. However, there was a general similarity of model for the evaluation of principals, using the district superintendents or assistant superintendents whose role was akin to that of the 'patch' adviser in England and Wales. If the role was similar, however, the career route to the post of district superintendent did not mirror that of the British counterpart.

In North America, initial principalship appointments are generally to small schools, often in the least attractive parts of the inner city. With time and experience the principal may expect to move to larger institutions in more desirable locations where, inevitably, better salaries are paid and where the use of terms such as 'magnet school' or 'lighthouse school' implies the existence of excellent quality and high prestige. From these key appointments, opportunities then exist for the principal to go 'downtown' to the district head office to assistant superintendent or superintendent posts. This, for the American principal, is a straight line of promotion in both career and salary terms. Although in England and Wales some primary heads seek transfer to advisory or inspectorial posts, few secondary headteachers apply because, in salary terms, it is not seen as 'promotion'. This will be a key issue when the model for headteacher appraisal is addressed later in this chapter.

The ACAS Report establishes a starting position

Before the production of the ACAS *Report of the Appraisal/Training Working Group* in 1986 (hereafter called the 'ACAS Report') a number of headteachers had been experimenting with a variety of models of appraisal, often as a result of attending management courses where the influence of industrial models was paramount. Some headteachers allowed themselves to be appraised by officers, advisers, governors, subordinates, peers or a combination of these. From these experiments some good practice emerged but there were also some disasters. The ACAS Report, in recommending the setting up of pilot studies to try out appraisal schemes, did set out for the first time the purposes and principles of headteacher appraisal. The ACAS Report should, therefore, be viewed as a foundation on which the six pilot studies in Croydon, Cumbria, Newcastle-upon-Tyne, Salford, Somerset and Suffolk were to build, with the aid of educational support grants.

The ACAS Report did not discuss in detail the headteacher model or process, apart from two specific references. However, in paragraph three, the purposes of appraisal for teachers must be understood to apply equally to headteachers. For headteachers, the purposes of appraisal could be to inform one or more of the following:

- career development and individual professional decisions
- decisions affecting the improvement of the school
- LEA management decisions about personnel and schools.

It will immediately be seen that the performance of the head is closely linked with the effectiveness of the school as a whole. Most of the pilot studies have emphasised the need for 'whole school' review or 'institutional self-evaluation' to be a prerequisite for both teacher and headteacher appraisal, recognising that an important end-product of appraisal is school improvement. This has been articulated clearly within the pilot studies where the individual development of headteachers has been linked to the notion of school improvement:

'The purpose is to benefit the learning of pupils by promoting effective leadership and management.' (Somerset LEA, 1988), and

'The fundamental purpose of the scheme is to achieve professional development for all headteachers and thereby enrich the provision for pupils and staff in all schools.' (Newcastle-upon-Tyne LEA, 1988).

The two specific references to headteacher appraisal within the ACAS Report occur in paragraph four where, within the scope of appraisal, the working group notes:

> 'we see all teachers including headteachers being covered' (by appraisal) and in paragraph five, which answers the question, 'Who appraises whom?': 'The appraisal of headteachers will be the responsibility of the CEO who shall appoint as appraiser an appropriate person with relevant experience as a headteacher, who will be required to consult with the designated inspector responsible for the school and the designated education officer.' The sentence which follows this paragraph was seen to apply equally to headteachers and teachers: 'The working group considers that, where necessary, each appraisal should benefit from a second informed opinion.'

One general principle which was accepted by all as being vital and applying equally to headteachers and teachers was the nature of the process: 'The working group understands appraisal ... as a continuous and systematic process.' The frequency of appraisal for headteachers was not specifically mentioned in the ACAS Report, but it was generally assumed that the reference in Annex A to the frequency of appraisal for 'all other categories' included headteachers, in which case the frequency of appraisal should be 'regularly after periods of not less than one year or greater than ... years.' Most pilot project teams assumed that the reasonable figure for '... years' was three and that, for headteachers, a triennial cycle of appraisal was both practical and appropriate.

The ACAS Report, tabled in June 1986, was the starting point for the six pilot LEAs which were selected in December 1986 by the Secretary of State and which began piloting appraisal between January and June 1987. The work of the pilot LEAs was further complicated by two pieces of legislation affecting teacher and headteacher appraisal. The salary scales and conditions of service imposed by the Secretary of State in 1986 overtook the ACAS recommendations but still included appraisal as a condition of service to be introduced following the promulgation of national guidelines drawing on the experience of the pilot studies. More significant for headteacher appraisal was the 1988 Education Reform Act. The 1986 Act required LEAs to introduce regular appraisal of teachers and headteachers but the 1988 Education Reform Act placed staff appointments, terminations, staffing levels, deployment and the monitoring of appraisal in the hands of governors. The experience of the pilot LEAs in the appraisal of headteachers will need to take account of the influence, inhibiting or otherwise, which the Local Management of Schools (LMS) will exercise over any schemes which the LEA might wish to introduce.

Who appraises the headteacher?

Although the ACAS Report places the responsibility for the selection of the headteacher's appraiser on the chief education officer, the stipulation that the appraiser must have relevant experience of headship inhibits CEOs in their choice. One headteacher professional association in the ACAS working group wished to have 'experience' further qualified by 'recent' which, if accepted, would have been even further restrictive of choice. It is very clear that a large number of LEAs will not be able to use the greater part of the advisory/inspectorial service to appraise heads if the 'relevant experience' principle is firmly applied.

In March 1986, the Committee of Heads of Educational Institutions (CHEI) put forward a discussion document outlining its members' thinking about the appraisal of heads and principals. Its main thrust was the establishment of a national task force of heads seconded for two or three years to become professional appraisers of headteachers throughout the country. This well-meaning suggestion not only ignored the problems which such appraisers would face in familiarising themselves with an unknown local context but it also failed to take account of their inability to facilitate agreed outcomes and to provide personal long-term support. Furthermore, few headteachers would be prepared to leave their schools for two or three years when so many fundamental changes are being introduced into our education system and even fewer governing bodies, with their greatly increased powers, would be likely to release headteachers when schools are being required to manage multiple changes.

What is true for a national task force is equally true for a local task force. Yet the CEO has a local decision to make. If secondment is out of the question, can use be made of retired heads? Professor Ted Wragg has certainly put this forward as a way out of the CEO's dilemma. Headteachers themselves have, in the main, preferred to be appraised by what they term 'live' heads. 'Live' heads are credible, they have a knowledge of and feel for the post of headship as it is happening now, not as it happened yesterday. This is one of the headteachers' main objections to being appraised by advisers or inspectors who have not been headteachers: that they will not appreciate problems of which they have had no previous experience.

Within the six pilot authorities a number of models have been tried out, giving the ACAS paragraph a variety of interpretations. This paragraph refers to 'one appraiser' appointed by the CEO yet later states that appraisal can benefit from a 'second informed opinion'. This has led some of the pilot LEAs to use two appraisers. What is clear is that most of the pilot LEAs are using peer appraisal as a significant part of their model. Headteachers in post are used as consultant heads to appraise colleagues, are placed on a panel of appraisers or accept that, as pilot heads being appraised, they, in turn, will be called upon to appraise others. In all cases an adviser, inspector or officer is used to inform or facilitate at some stage.

What has yet to be tested is how far headteachers may be required to participate in the appraisal of other headteachers. So far, all headteachers acting as appraisers have been volunteers. The conditions of service for headteachers (DES, 1987) refers only to a headteacher participating in his own appraisal:

Appraisal of headteacher

(21) (a) participating in any arrangements within an agreed national framework for the appraisal of *his performance* as headteacher.

Given the existence of a team of appraisers variously termed 'panel', 'volunteer', 'consultant' or 'associate', how are these matched to the individual heads who are to be appraised? In one LEA, where two appraisers are involved, one, an adviser, is designated by the CEO while the other, a panel head, is selected by the headteacher. In another LEA, where two headteachers are appraisers, one in a key role, the second in a supporting one, the headteacher may declare a 'negative preference' from the list of available headteachers where personal or professional incompatibility is likely to exist. Perhaps the phrase 'negative preference' could be more sensitively expressed by asking that CEOs should treat sympathetically requests from headteachers for alternative appraisers - again where the appraisal of the head by a particular appraiser would not be professionally productive. Peer appraisal produces its own problems in matching appraisers to appraisees, especially in small urban LEAs where, with falling rolls, schools are competing more fiercely for a share of the pupil population. This is particularly true in the secondary phase. In a compact borough, where all secondary schools may be within 15 minutes driving time of each other, the severity of catchment competition may persuade the LEA to have a professional appraiser with headship experience within its staff development team. However, in the shire counties where, with careful matching, catchment competition can be avoided, peer appraisal is a professionally rewarding experience for the appraiser as well as the appraisee.

Whenever peer appraisers are used in headship appraisal, LEAs will have to make important decisions about the criteria for including heads in appraiser teams. Will all headteachers, irrespective of length of experience, be expected to appraise others? If so, where do heads in their induction year, and heads whose performance has been recognised as marginal, stand? How are the successful yet 'maverick' heads to be fitted into appraisal teams - heads who succeed yet break all the rules and are the bane of the administrator's life? Should headteachers undertake an apprenticeship as a 'support appraiser' before being given the more responsible and onerous task of 'key appraiser'? What loading can appraising heads take if they are not only to appraise but also to provide support afterwards to ensure that appraisal is a 'continuous and systematic process'? CEOs will need to consider the simple fact that, given a triennial cycle of appraisal for head-teachers, given that each head has two appraisers to act as checks and bal-ances and, if every headteacher in the LEA is used as an appraiser, then each year every single head will be either appraising another head or being appraised. Will CEOs, governors and the headteachers themselves accept an appraisal programme where heads are simultaneously appraising as well as being appraised? Yet, if an LEA has identified from 10 to 20 per cent of its headteachers as 'beginning heads', 'retiring heads', 'mavericks' or 'mar-ginal performers', there is an immediate logistical problem affecting pro-gramming. This problem would be even further exacerbated by a biennial cycle of appraisal. What of the urban LEAs, few in number perhaps, where the turnover rate per annum for headteachers is as high as 50 per cent? If headteachers are identified as sensitive yet thoroughly professional apprai-sers of their colleagues, are they likely to be over-used by the LEA? Head-teachers who have been identified as good committee members have tended to suffer in this way. Now, with LMS and stricter governor control, will head-teachers be released to join elite teams of LEA appraisers while still run-ning their schools? In the long term, when appraisal becomes institutionalised, more refined selection procedures for headship will in-clude an examination of the potential of candidates to appraise colleague heads. Appraisal will be part of the aspiring head's management armoury. But the mid-term will bring with it problems which will no doubt be solved in different ways by LEAs, each according to their means and needs.

Where, then, do LEA officers, advisers and inspectors stand in relation to the appraisal of headteachers? The ACAS paragraph places them in a consultative role, though it is unclear as to what exactly 'consult' means in this context. The six pilot LEAs have used LEA personnel in many differ-ent roles. None has clearly defined an LEA representative as the line-man-ager of the headteacher or, to use the ACAS term, the 'immediate supervisor'. Most LEAs accept the two parallel lines of a head's responsi-bility to the CEO and to the governors through the chairperson. In one pilot LEA, the key appraiser was an adviser, not necessarily with headship ex-perience though assisted by a practising head. In another pilot LEA an ad-viser was the single appraiser. In two LEAs the appraising headteacher(s) used an LEA officer/adviser to provide contextual information, to agree the appraisal report and to assist with follow-up. In another LEA, peer apprai-sal based on professional partnership was validated by an LEA adviser. All have involved elements of LEA consultation in a variety of ways.

Where LEA advisers/inspectors have been used as appraisers, clear role conflict has been experienced both by the headteacher and by the adviser. The double professional style of advising and inspecting has been further complicated by individuals now having to 'wear a third hat', that of the appraiser, requiring new skills and different sensitivities. As advisers will need to adopt a more inspectorial role in order to monitor the national curriculum, the tension between the developmental role of the head's appraiser and the accountability role of the LEA inspector will certainly increase.

A further problem in some LEAs has been the conflict or imbalance between the subject and pastoral responsibilities of the advisory service. Officers and advisers are of inestimable value to appraiser heads in giving background and contextual information about the appraised head and the school. Where the adviser strategy has placed the emphasis on a subject-dominated approach with a very limited use of 'patch' advisers (although advisory support has been very satisfactory during the pilot), the level of support for headteachers could not be sustained were the scheme extended to the whole LEA. The success of the involvement of the advisory service in headteacher appraisal will not rest solely on previous experience of headship but will be very much affected by the number of schools for which each adviser will be responsible. A survey of LEAs, their total number of establishments set against their total advisory/inspectorial staffing will show widely differing ratios.

If advisers are not used as appraisers, they will still have a vital role to play in monitoring the outcomes of an individual head's appraisal, providing the resources needed to meet those outcomes, giving support and continuing recognition through follow-up visits.

How is the headteacher to be appraised?

Now that some of the issues emerging from consideration of the selection of appraisers have been addressed, it may be valuable to discuss the components of the appraisal process and how these function in practice. Being broadly similar to the teacher appraisal process, the headteacher process in its simplest form has four main elements:

Initial review meeting between appraiser(s) and appraisee

Data collection

Appraisal interview
Target setting
Appraisal record produced

Follow-up discussions/meeting between appraiser and appraisee
Professional development activities

Expressed in this sequential form, appraisal may not be seen as 'a continuous and systematic process'. To reinforce this concept, some of the pilot LEAs have shown their appraisal components in a cyclical form (Figure 4:1, Somerset LEA, 1988)

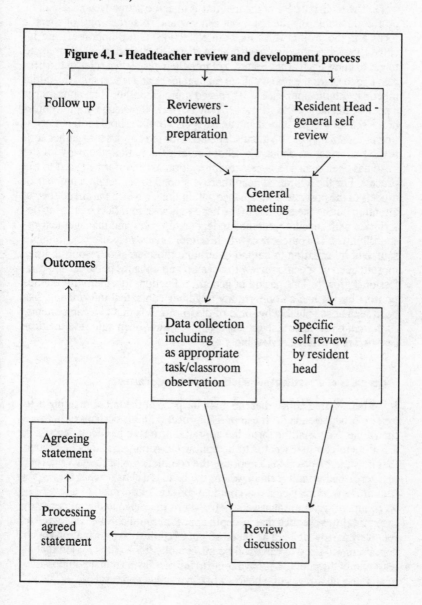

Figure 4.1 - Headteacher review and development process

Starting the headteacher appraisal process

Although the initial review meeting would be seen as the start of the process, the appraisee and the appraiser both need to undertake preparatory work. The main purpose of the meeting is to agree a broad agenda, to draw up the timetable for the appraisal process and to agree areas of specific focus and the ground rules for data collection. If two appraisers are involved, they may not know each other well and, if they can meet beforehand to get to know each other better, to agree their respective roles in the process and to share their views about management and leadership, the initial meeting with the appraisee will proceed more smoothly. If an appraiser is a peer head and not the school's 'patch' adviser, knowledge of the context of the school will be limited and an early visit to the school for familiarisation purposes may pay dividends. The need for the appraiser to gather contextual information about the school before the initial meeting with the head has been seen as a necessary foundation for an informed start to the process. For the appraisee head there is a need to reflect on a number of aspects of the post and performance within the job which may need special attention during the appraisal. The head may wish to reflect on the job description with specific reference to leadership roles and management responsibilities. The outcome of 'whole school' review may also be a valuable source of information to help to determine those areas of responsibilities most in need of specific review to develop and enhance personal and professional growth. This period of general reflection, together with the appraisers having had an opportunity to gather contextual information, has been seen as so valuable by some of the pilot LEAs that two components, *contextual preparation* and *general self review* have been built into the process before the initial review meeting.

What parts of a headteacher's job should be appraised?

It has been stated above that the main purpose of the initial meeting is to agree a broad agenda for the appraisal process. This is perhaps easier said than done. Now that the form the appraisal is to take has been described, it is time to consider what is to be appraised. Although it may be argued that it would be possible to appraise the complete job of the headteacher of a very small primary school, where the head is a class teacher for 80 per cent of the working week, this could not be said of the head of a large 11-18 community comprehensive school, where the range and complexity of responsibilities are such that in-depth appraisal could only be conducted in relatively narrow fields. The sheer weight of contextual information which appraisers will need to carry will be formidable. It is for this reason that at least four of the pilot LEAs have come to the conclusion that it is impossible to appraise all aspects of a head's work in a single appraisal cycle. The alternative is to examine in depth certain areas of focus - normally three. What is now crucial is how these areas of focus are selected. Some of the pilot LEAs have, during training programmes, produced a matrix of headteacher tasks and responsibilities, linked with job descriptions, and these have been used as a basis for the selection of specific areas for appraisal.

There are many problems in what seems a simple choice of three areas of focus. Are areas simply selected by three individuals acting independently? If the areas are negotiated with the appraisee, can 'no go' areas be omitted? Will appraisers choose areas in which they consider they have some expertise, irrespective of their value to the appraisee? Should areas of focus which the LEA considers vital for appraisal be introduced into the agenda? If so, how can this be done without appraisal moving towards marginal performance review? Although areas of focus can be examined and the head will be seen to be performing a given task, how is the quality of that performance to be evaluated? Who will decide the criteria or performance indicators which will be linked with a specific responsibility? Within some of the pilot LEAs, it has also been suggested that specific areas of focus might be linked to recent research on what constitutes effective schools and the management strategies that appear to promote such schools (for example, the recent work of Mortimore *et al*, (*Open Books*, 1988) which examined effective leadership and management in primary schools). What is clear is that consideration of which parts of a head's work need to be appraised is not only vital but produces many potential difficulties.

How is information about the head's performance to be collected?

When, at the initial meeting, the areas of focus have been decided, the appraisers and appraisee have to decide what data are to be collected and, more important, how they are to he collected. A wide range of methods of collecting data is being used to gather information for headteacher appraisal. The following list, which is not exhaustive, illustrates some of the techniques:

- classroom observation - particularly for primary headteachers with a class responsibility
- task observation - the observation of managerial tasks associated with headship, for example, chairing meetings, contributing to meetings, 'shadowing'
- review of relevant school documents - for example, the staff handbook, reports to governors
- consultation with staff - the identification of the staff to be involved as agreed at the initial meeting

- consultation with governors where relevant to an area of focus - for example, boundary management

- consultation with LEA officer/adviser - the provision of relevant information for the areas of focus is one important role the LEA plays in the process

- consultation with parents - again where relevant to an area of focus such as 'external relations'

- tour of premises and grounds - either guided or independent as agreed

- self-appraisal - a key feature in all pilot LEAs. Paragraph five of the ACAS Report states that 'each appraisal should be preceded and informed by self-appraisal'. This is regarded as a key stage in the process and detailed advice is given to appraisees as to how their self-appraisal may be conducted.

As more experience is gained in data collection, each of the nine techniques for gathering information listed above reveals issues and problems which will have to be addressed and answered to the satisfaction of all involved in the process. Two illustrations of these issues, touching on task observation and staff consultation, can be included here.

Task observation was included in the process for non-teaching heads so that consistency between the appraisal of teachers and headteachers was maintained. It was accepted that, just as teachers are observed at work in the classroom, so, too, should headteachers be observed at work carrying out their management functions. The key issue here is the identification of managerial tasks which are both observable and worth observing. Although 'observing an assembly' led by the head has been often suggested as a typical task to be observed, a group from the pilot co-ordinators' conference, in addressing this question, felt that only three areas were appropriate for task observation: appointment and management of staff, relationships with parents, and relationships with the governing body. A further issue which has not been explored in depth is the agreement of the criteria or performance indicators to be used in evaluating the task being observed. Clearly, just as instruments have been developed for classroom observation, so, too, will instruments need to be developed for task observation if it is to be a valid component of data collection.

When staff have been involved in contributing professional information touching on the management performance of the head, the first questions to be answered are: Which staff are involved? Who chooses them? Are prompt questions shared beforehand with the appraisee? Are staff sources of information to be revealed to the head? Do appraisers feed back to the head all the information they have gathered from staff? What is clear from the experience of the pilots is that staff involved in providing information for their head's appraisal have feelings of professional discomfort bordering on disloyalty when discussing their head's management or leadership practice with an outsider. It is obvious that teaching staff will need training for this and an established 'code of practice' will need to be drawn up to protect both staff and heads.

The appraisal interview

The appraisal interview is seen as the central part of the appraisal process, for it is at this meeting that the appraisers and appraisee will pool, share and discuss the information which they have gathered and agree an action plan for the future which will assist both the head's and the school's development. It must not be forgotten that appraisal is a cyclical process and, therefore, the appraisal interview is not the end stage in the process. Regular follow-up sessions either by appraisers or LEA advisers, or both, are necessary if appraisal is to be seen as a continuous and systematic process.

It should be noted here that only two of the pilot LEAs use the term, 'appraisal interview', for this stage of the process. The other pilot LEAs prefer either 'discussion' or 'dialogue' to describe what is essentially a balanced, two-way review of a professional's performance to identify, explain and resolve issues together.

The appraisal interview for a headteacher may take many hours and, for all involved, new skills and different professional sensitivities will be needed. Training in these skills, which will be transferable to other areas of management, are essential and cannot be taken for granted. Where two appraisers are used, the appraisal interview becomes a 'three-cornered' discussion, requiring different interview strategies. With the length of time involved in the appraisal interview, good quality note-taking and summarising are vital if professionally satisfactory conclusions are to be reached. It has been found that there has been a positive advantage in having two appraisers, with one chairing and leading sections of the discussion while the other has taken notes, enabling summarised conclusions to be agreed quickly and effectively. With appraisers having responsibility for specific areas of focus, the roles of 'chair' and 'note-taker' have been interchangeable at different stages of the appraisal interview.

The outcome of the appraisal interview is an action plan duly recorded with targets detailed to assist the professional development of the headteacher. The appraisal record so produced has been called the 'agreed statement' in three of the pilot LEAs to illustrate that it is not a 'report on' a headteacher but a mutually agreed plan for development, with the appraisee having a large measure of ownership of the document. The action plan will include 'contracts for action' not only involving the appraised headteacher but also the appraisers with, in some cases, the CEO's representative contracting delivery of resources on behalf of the LEA. It is essential that, if targets provisionally agreed at the appraisal interview have resource implications for the LEA, the CEO's representative must discuss and agree these before they can be included in the appraisal record.

All the pilot LEAs have addressed a series of questions about the distribution, access, use and life of the appraisal record. Their answers have not always shown a consistency of response, with much depending on the professional climate and practice in individual LEAs. Only one LEA suggested that the appraisal record should be stored outside the school within the LEA head office but most agreed that the CEO or an agreed representative of the CEO should have access to the document, which follows the ACAS Report principle for teachers which states that 'Appraisal interview reports ... be available to appraisers and officers authorised by the CEO.' The main use of the appraisal record will be to identify the professional development needs of the headteacher and enable the LEA to provide better informed headteacher references when necessary. How far the appraisal record of headteachers will assist the LEA in making management decisions or in succession planning remains as yet unclear. Much will depend on the content and quality of appraisal records and how far they can be monitored and moderated to ensure consistency across a broad band of appraisers. It is generally agreed that, like the teachers' appraisal records, the life of a headteacher's appraisal record would continue until the next appraisal record had been completed. The right of retention or withdrawal from the head's file at this point would rest with the appraised head.

Governors and the appraisal of headteachers

It is perhaps appropriate at this point to consider the role which governors may or may not play in the appraisal of headteachers. Although headteachers have a dual line of responsibility to both the CEO and to the governing body, it has not been accepted that in conventional line-management terms the headteacher reports to the chair of governors.

Little reference is made in the ACAS Report to governing bodies. There is one reference to the need for the selected pilot authorities to consider the 'distinctive features of aided schools whose governing bodies employ the teachers'. Other references to governors are conspicuous by their absence. The Report was of course written pre-LMS and before the powers and responsibilities of governing bodies had been significantly increased by legislation. Within the pilot LEAs there has again been a difference of practice with either the exclusion of governors from a process which is essentially seen as for, and carried out by, professionals or the involvement of governors at the discretion of the headteacher. Where appraisees have exercised their discretion, governors have been involved in a variety of ways:

- appraisers have briefed governing bodies about the appraisal process before the start of the head's appraisal
- governors have provided appraisers with relevant information about the head's performance, either collectively or individually
- appraisers have observed headteachers contributing to governors' meetings
- chair of governors has been given access to the appraisal record
- appraised heads have reported to the governors on their own appraisal in the presence of their appraisers
- appraisers have reported to the governors on the head's appraisal in the presence of the headteacher.

Although governors have often played significant parts in the appraisal of pilot heads, it has normally been where confident and successful heads have been willing to exercise their discretion. There is still much concern both within pilot schools and in non-pilot schools about the role of governors, both as a body and as represented by the chair, in both the appraisal of heads and in the even more contentious matter of access to appraisal records. Most involved in the pilot projects, and this includes a strong, unanimous voice from the professional associations, agree that the appraisal record is largely 'raw professional data' - produced with a professional confidentiality and requiring professional interpretation. Governors, as lay people, are not seen as having the expertise to analyse and interpret this data. Reports on the performance of teachers and headteachers can be called for, in the normal way, by requests to the headteacher or the LEA. Both may draw on data from the appraisal records to inform these reports when necessary.

For LEAs a more important issue will be the extent to which governing bodies, with their new powers, will be prepared to support the scheme for headteacher appraisal which the LEA will introduce in accordance with the national guidelines. Will governors happily accept the regular disappearance from their school of their headteacher to another part of LEA to appraise another head if peer appraisal were the preferred scheme? Will governing bodies with much industrial representation prefer to buy in management consultants to appraise their head rather than accept an LEA scheme which they do not understand because it does not carry out the functions which they experience in industry? These are but two of the questions which will begin to surface as LMS establishes itself.

Appraisal - a systematic and continuous process

In many industrial models, appraisal is seen as an annual 'happening' - a 'one off'. One pilot LEA, Somerset, accepting the importance of language, both in terms of emotive as well as of semantic understanding, preferred to use the term 'Review and Development' for appraisal. This use is well supported in the work of the ACAS research unit (James, 1988) where appraisal is defined as only taking a 'rear mirror' view of an individual's performance and where the need is to project forward as well as to look back. The preferred term in this research work was PRD - Performance Review and Development.

The 1986 ACAS Report emphasised that appraisal must be a *systematic and continuous process*. The 'frequency' principle has been a major consideration, hotly debated during the pilot studies. The majority of pilot studies recommended a triennial cycle for headteachers, while the DES Circular of Guidance to LEAs of 12 August 1988 suggested that a two- or three-year cycle of appraisal was appropriate for headteachers, with annual appraisal for teachers. Certainly the teachers' professional associations would strongly endorse the principle of parity in the frequency of appraisal of teachers and headteachers. Annual appraisal is not realistic or sustainable for headteachers unless it becomes a perfunctory and sterile process. The same might be said about an annual frequency for teachers. For these reasons a biennial cycle of appraisal may be the best for headteachers as well as teachers. A biennial cycle would ensure that appraisal is 'systematic and continuous', would show the teacher and headteacher schemes as having parity. In cost terms it would make a considerable saving over an annual cycle and, above all, it would still be professionally consistent and credible.

Whatever the frequency ordered by the DES Regulations there is still the need for follow-up sessions to be built in, either with the appraiser or the appropriate LEA adviser. Within a school the appraiser of any teacher, including deputy heads, will be within the establishment in daily contact, with the appraiser having regular opportunities to provide both informal and formal support. Targets can be monitored or modified, developmental activities can be arranged or facilitated by the appraiser. For the headteacher appraisee with external appraisers, unless formal follow-up is arranged and accepted as an integral part of the process, the headteacher can remain isolated, unsupported and unrecognised once the appraisal interview has been completed.

Outstanding issues

The work on headteacher appraisal in the six pilot LEAs has at the time of writing been continuing for less than two years for some and less than a year for others. Experience is therefore limited, particularly in assessing the outcome of appraisal on the effectiveness of the headteacher. Only time will tell how much the appraisal of the head has benefited the children's learning or contributed to the development of the teaching staff.

Meanwhile, there are a number of process issues which further experience over the next few years must resolve. Among these are:

- locating responsibility for ensuring the headteacher's targets are set and met
- defining the role of governors
- agreeing access to and the use of appraisal records
- deciding the qualifications for headteacher appraisers
- providing initial training and 'top up' training for all headteachers
- setting up appropriate 'appeals' machinery
- ensuring that the constraints of time do not inhibit the developmental process
- establishing a code of practice for data collection and an appropriate instrument for task observation.

Although this clearly implies that there is still much work to be done, the headteachers in the pilot schools have not only successfully tried out approaches to headteacher appraisal but have also benefited themselves from the experience. Perhaps the last word should go to headteachers who have been through the appraisal process:

'I wouldn't have missed it. I have enjoyed it ... it was worthwhile, demanding and exhausting.'

'Some of my colleague headteachers may feel a little bit apprehensive about going through the whole appraisal process, but what we have to say to ourselves is - what is in it for the children? What is in it for the school? If at the end of the day we're better heads, and because our colleague teachers, likewise, are going through the process themselves, the education of the children will be so much better and the school will be a better institution.'

Chapter 5

Piloting Teacher Appraisal in an Outer London Borough

Maeve Willis

It is not quite clear whether it was a critic or a wit who described Croydon as 'the Dallas of the South', but it is an odd expression. It manages at one and the same time to deny the town its long and interesting history and to invest its readiness to involve itself in new ideas with the superficiality of a modern soap opera. In fact, Croydon was granted a market charter in the middle ages, it boasts sixteenth century almshouses in the centre of the town and has two Archbishops' palaces, one now an independent girls' school and the other The Royal School of Church Music. The Brighton Road, now a busy shopping thoroughfare, once carried the fashionable throng from the Prince Regent's London across the Downs to his Pavilion on the south coast. There are links with the East India Company and the roads in one area provide a roll of nineteenth century Indian Army Officers with echoes of the Mutiny.

Croydon has been an education authority in its own right since LEAs were first established and has almost a century of experience. In 1965, the reorganisation of local government in Greater London enlarged the town to include Coulsdon and Purley, a move never wholly accepted by those who still think of themselves as living in Surrey and who remember their education service being run from Kingston. It is now a long thin borough touching the Inner London Education Authority in the north and Surrey in the south. It is bordered east and west by the London Boroughs of Bromley, Merton and Sutton.

The landscape of the town, particularly in the centre, has changed radically over the last 30 years, with new road systems, post-war housing developments and new public buildings, including the Fairfield Halls, shopping precincts and modern office blocks. There are well maintained parks and gardens, good restaurants, alternative theatre and a first class concert hall. From his office, the director of education - and many of his staff - can look down on the Jubilee Gardens, flowers, fountains and a fine Henry Moore. Croydon is 15 minutes by rail from central London, 30 minutes from Gatwick and less than an hour from the coast. In many ways Croydon is not unlike its neighbours but boundaries have a way of defining differences. It may not be Dallas but it has its own distinctive quality.

In the council's annual report for 1987/88, published in January 1989, the leader of the council, Sir Peter Bowness, comments that, 'while the way in which local government operates is again undergoing change ... the future for Croydon as a borough has never looked brighter'. Among many aspects of the council's work to which he refers is the education service, which he describes as continuing 'to provide a first class service as well as a focus for pioneering developments in the curriculum and assessment which are to be implemented on a national basis'.

Change and development are the key words. Change is a fact of life and nowhere more so, it seems, than in education over the past 20 years. Teachers, to their credit, have faced it and have dealt with it successfully but there is a feeling today that there is more of it about, that the demands are increasing and that the deadlines get ever closer. Demographic patterns, coupled with legislation that is an expression of different educational and social philosophies, both underline these changes and demand a speedy response.

The situation in Croydon and the background against which teacher appraisal is being introduced are not untypical but for several reasons they have their own distinctive character. In the first place, the fall in pupil numbers has been one of the highest in the country - 41 per cent in 12 years in the 11-16 age range. Second, local policy under the former director of education, Donald Naismith, was imbued with a pioneering spirit that led to involvement in a variety of projects including TVEI, CPVE, pupil assessment at 7, 11 and 14, GRIDS, DEA and other approaches to 'whole school' evaluation and school effectiveness, management training for headteachers, profiling and records of achievement and a massive investment in IT. The dramatic fall in pupil numbers has resulted not only in the closure of schools but in a rationalisation of the existing provision at secondary level. The dual system of comprehensive schools offering two routes through secondary education by way of linked 11-14/14-18 schools and 11-16 schools has been replaced by a single system of county 11-16 schools with separate post-16 provision at one of two sixth form colleges or at Croydon College of Further and Higher Education. Three voluntary-aided schools continue to provide for pupils 11-18 (see Figure 5.1).

A third factor was the reorganisation of the inspectorate with an emphasis on its inspectorial and monitoring roles which made for a significant change in the relationship between inspectors and schools.

In an uncertain world we cling to the idea of past stability and the myth of a golden age perhaps to protect ourselves against what we conceive to be the harsh realities of change - and this is understandable. Stability and continuity of tried and successful practice provide reassurance, a firm basis on which to work, but they also breed complacency, staleness and inertia.

Figure 5.1 - London Borough of Croydon

Number of Schools

Nursery	4
Primary	100
Secondary	23: (11-16) 18; (11-18) 3;
	(6th Form College) 2
Special	6

Number of Teachers (FTE)	2266
Number of Pupils	41330
Population of Croydon (based on 1981 Census)	319200

Change offers challenge and the stimulus that helps us to deal with it. It offers the attraction of new ideas, the opportunity to review what we value, to look at our work from a new perspective. Often it is less radical than it appears and only requires us to adopt new approaches to the same thing, to capitalise on what we are already doing. It can inspire a sense of adventure and the energy that comes with new endeavours but, if the change is fundamental, there is a danger of creating the kind of anxiety and loss of confidence that makes one retreat into inaction and adopt negative attitudes as a form of protection.

As always, the balance is important. The tightrope walker needs the reassurance of constant practice and established techniques as he takes the first step on to the high wire. In some ways, though, each performance is a new experience. He cannot afford to ignore the possibility of the unexpected and he must be ready to deal with it. The hazard of a drop into the ring below is a necessary stimulus to success.

There is another myth about change - namely, that it applies to us and to no one else. It is true that the factors referred to earlier - falling rolls, school closures and reorganisation - have meant a great deal of change for Croydon teachers but, to varying degrees, this has been true for colleagues in many other parts of the country. It is also true that legislation affecting the curriculum, management and the role of governors applies nationally, but locally and even at school level there is a tendency to perceive it only as it applies to ourselves and to our immediate colleagues - something dreamed up by the LEA or possibly as the whim of an over-innovative head.

Into this scene comes appraisal, either as saviour or as necessary evil. It is certainly not the latter but neither should it be seen as a cure-all, a problem solver for all seasons. Its great virtue is that it can facilitate change. It provides opportunities for discussing change, seeing what it means for the individual and the school and finding ways of dealing with it. It is sad, but not surprising, that the introduction of appraisal should have been met with such hostility and suspicion. Some of this is peculiar to Croydon, in part because of the emphasis which has been placed on the assessment, evaluation and monitoring of pupil, teacher and school performance and that of the authority as a whole. Every area has its own sensitivities and tensions, however, and they may well produce the same reactions. In this respect, Croydon's experience as part of the pilot project should be of interest to others setting out along the same road.

At the outset, several factors had to be taken into account: first, there were the usual tensions between the education office and the schools, often arising from different perspectives and some failures of communication. There are those who have forgotten the way schools think and others who are unaware of the pressures under which LEAs have to work. Shared understanding would help. Second, despite the 1986 ACAS agreement on appraisal, there was the attitude in 1987 of some of the teachers' associations and the reluctance of others to rock the boat. Third, there was locally a long-running disagreement between teachers and the LEA about assessment testing and the use to which results might be put. This was exacerbated by the statement in Croydon's brochure on appraisal that there was a link between teacher appraisal and pupil performance. Taken out of context this was dismissed as an attempt to concentrate only on measurable outcomes, to neglect other aspects of a teacher's work and to introduce payment by results. It may be worth quoting two of the relevant passages:

(i) Croydon's approach to appraisal proceeds from the assumption that 'no useful or credible judgement can be made about a teacher's classroom effectiveness or performance without taking into account an assessment of the learning achieved by the teacher's pupils'.

(ii) It forms no part of Croydon's argument that education can or should be reduced to a series of measurable activities. It does, however, hold that demonstrable pupil attainment cannot be disregarded if a system of teacher appraisal is to fulfil one of its central purposes of promoting the effectiveness of the teacher's work in the classroom. Successful teaching cannot be separated from successful learning.

Clearly, questions are raised here which are worth asking and which cannot he dismissed without proper consideration. Behind all these factors lay the shadow of two years of industrial action and a deep suspicion of the attitudes that seemed to be encapsulated in Sir Keith Joseph's reference to the 'weeding out of incompetent teachers'. It was not the most propitious moment to introduce an initiative requiring teachers to evaluate their performance, discuss it, warts and all, with 'their immediate supervisor' (ACAS), possibly the headteacher, and produce a record of what had been said. Propitious or not, there was a project to be undertaken, it seemed to have merits, not least the fact that the employers and all the teachers' associations had agreed to it in principle, and there was a time limit in which to complete it. The question was how to change the climate and to increase teachers' awareness of the benefits of appraisal.

There was commitment and drive at a senior level in the authority, an essential starting point but not enough. In the first place, the approach had to be positive, based on honesty and openness and seen to be so. Second, there had to be teacher involvement in managing the project and in contributing to its development. One condition was met by appointing a secondary head and two deputies, one secondary and one primary, to form the project team; the other was met by the team's deliberate policy right from the outset to give teachers a central role in the development process. Those concerned have valued this policy and the opportunities it has given them, but it has had the effect of distancing the LEA and leaving the question of their appropriate involvement so far unanswered. It is only now, in the final stages of the project, that this issue is being addressed more seriously.

Following its own initial training, the team began its work by inviting heads to one of a series of small group discussions. Their support was essential. The response was encouraging, though not everyone came and some made it plain that they had no intention of being involved. It was understood on each occasion that appraisal was neither to be mentioned nor discussed unless it was generally agreed by those present. Despite this rather strange situation, it was possible to discuss ways in which heads formed impressions of their staff, the basis on which they currently wrote references on them and recommended them for INSET or promotion. Were there better ways of doing this, ways in which the staff themselves could be involved? It was not much but it was a beginning and two things emerged. One was that, in attending management courses, heads were already learning about appraisal schemes and in various ways introducing them into their schools. The other was that, in clarifying job descriptions, writing school development plans, establishing policies for staff development and encouraging target setting, they were dealing with many of the elements essential to appraisal. The door was not quite open but at least it was ajar.

The formation of a local steering group (LSG) as an advisory and consultative body was the next step. Invitations were extended to all the teachers' associations, the chief inspector, the director of in-service training, the principal staffing officer (schools), the diocesan schools commission

(Roman Catholic) and the diocesan board of education (Church of England). The project team are members of the group and the area HMI attends as an observer. The meetings are chaired by Professor Michael Eraut from the department of education, University of Sussex.

An early decision of the LSG was the setting up of task groups to investigate various aspects of appraisal: classroom observation, headteacher appraisal, the link, already referred to, between teacher appraisal and pupil performance, the position of voluntary-aided schools. Teachers were invited to join these groups, two of which involved working with Professor Eraut or one of his colleagues, and to report on their findings to the LSG. At the same time, it was decided to form a team of associate trainers who would be able to support the project team when pilot work actually began. All these activities were valuable and important in their own right but they had the added advantage of increasing the number of those who had a clearer understanding of what appraisal meant and could carry that message back to their own schools. The teachers involved were all volunteers and they rapidly became interested in and enthusiastic about the work they were doing. Schools, however, were still reluctant to commit themselves. At the same time, they wanted to know what was on offer, to have some of their questions answered and to express their anxieties. The team was happy to address these issues and to open the door a little wider. They met teachers informally, spoke at staff meetings, organised awareness-raising Baker days, made endless telephone calls and drank a lot of discursive coffee. There was a newsletter and a small but informative introductory pamphlet. As a result, in July 1987, four schools said they were prepared to accept training and do some pre-pilot work. This gave the team an opportunity to try out training strategies on a small scale and to learn from their mistakes without doing too much damage. Though this informal involvement with teachers was a response to a situation rather than a policy decision, it was, as it turned out, a very valuable exercise.

This interim period was also used to offer training to some of the inspectors and advisers. This had a number of benefits, not the least of which was enhanced credibility both for appraisal and for the project team itself.

The project's original remit was to pilot appraisal in four primary schools and two secondary schools. The team had always been clear that this should be done on a voluntary basis and when an invitation to be involved was sent out in the summer term 1988 the response was greater than could be sensibly handled. After consultation with a sub-committee of the LSG, 19 schools were selected (12 primary, 6 secondary and 1 sixth form college) and 15 heads (10 primary and 5 secondary) said they were willing to be appraised. Work began in the autumn term. It is always possible that an unexpected gust of wind could slam the door but, for the moment, it is open.

One of the team's basic principles was that training should be provided for all, for appraisees as well as appraisers. It seemed unreasonable to expect two people to engage in an activity and for only one of them to know the rules of the game. At the same time, it was recognised that it was not going to be possible to offer the same amount of training to everybody. In all but two cases, where the team was working with senior management only, whole schools were involved. The programme began with an introductory module. Experience has shown this to be an essential opening strategy. It enables the trainers to introduce themselves, to describe their approach, outline the training programme and, above all, to allay anxieties. It need take no more than an hour, less if necessary, and should be timed so as to contribute to the success of subsequent training without overburdening the staff. Too long an interval allows interest to flag but a compressed programme, including twilight sessions, stuns rather than stimulates.

The main training packages were as follows:

For the whole staff:

- two after-school modules - directed time.
- one Baker day (see Figures 5.2 and 5.3).

For appraisers, including heads:

- An additional 2.5 days residential course to consider the process in more detail and to receive initial skills training.

For heads only:

- A further 2.5 days residential course to deal more specifically with their own appraisal and to consider the management implications of appraisal.

The three possible models in Figure 5.2 are a reflection of the schools' own calendars. Each has its advantages and disadvantages but it seems clear that models A and C are likely to be more successful than B.

From the outset the team worked within the principles outlined in ACAS, in particular the understanding that appraisal is a 'continuous and systematic process intended to help individual teachers with their professional development and career planning, and to ensure that the in-service training and deployment of teachers matches the complementary needs of individual teachers and the schools.'

The process adopted (see Figure 5.4) is not unlike that piloted in other LEAs, though some of the language may be different. In general the model has proved to be acceptable and workable. The concept of continuity is well understood and recognised as being important, referring as it does to the appraiser/appraisee relationship and to the belief that appraisal is a continuous process and not merely an interview. It is, however, difficult to manage, particularly in secondary schools where staffing structures and cross-curricular responsibilities do not lend themselves to the estab-

Figure 5.2 - 'Whole School' Training (3): Training Models/Packages/Sessions

Training Packages	Time	Model A	Model B	Model C
TP1 Process Purposes	1.5 hrs		Session 1	Session 1
TP2 2a Jobs	1.5 hrs		Session 2	
2b Material 2c Targets Assumptions/ Constraints	1.5 hrs 0.5 hrs	Baker Day		Baker Day
TP3 Regular Professional Contact	1/1.5 hrs	Session 1	Baker Day	
TP4 Appraisal Interview	1.5/2 hrs	Session 2		Session 2

Figure 5.3 - 'Whole School' Training (1) : training packages

Introduction (Ice Breaker)		1.5 hrs
TP1	**Awareness Raising**	
	Context	
	Purpose +	1.5 hrs
	Process	
	Outcomes	
	Issues	
TP2	**Initial Discussion - Agree the Ground Rules**	
2a	*Job definition*	1.5 hrs
2b	*Possible material for discussion*	1.5 hrs
2c	*Targets* }	
	Assumptions and constraints }	0.5 hrs
TP3	**Regular Professional Contact**	
	Regular informal professional dialogue	
	Classroom observation	1/1.5 hrs *
	Collection of appropriate information	
	Interim review (if appropriate)	
TP4	**Appraisal Interview**	
	Pre-interview meeting	
	Preparation/*self-review*	
	Interview - structure and skills	1.5/2 hrs *
	Record	
	Outcomes	
	Follow-up	

Notes: * The timing of the training packages depends on the training model used.

+ Particular attention is paid to the items italicised.

Figure 5.4 - Croydon Teacher Appraisal Pilot Project
The Appraisal Process

APPRAISAL is a CONTINUOUS PROCESS - not an annual interview

The Appraisal Process: Elements of Each Cycle

1. Initial discussion - agree the ground rules:

    Job definition (main areas of responsibility)
    Material for discussion
    Targets
    Assumptions and constraints

2. Regular professional contact:

    Regular, informal, professional dialogue
    Classroom observation
    Collection of appropriate information

3. Pre-interview meeting:

4. Interview preparation:

    Self-review by appraisee
    Collection of information by appraiser

5. Appraisal interview:

    Review
    Development
    Planning - the year ahead

6. Agreed record

7. Appropriate follow-up

lishment of a natural professional relationship with an assigned appraiser, however carefully chosen. Where it already exists, as with the head of a major department, it works well. Where it does not, it has to be invented and this can be onerous and less satisfactory.

The notion of 'line management' does not fit any more comfortably into a large primary school where the head will find it difficult to appraise all the staff, particularly if regulations require this to be undertaken annually. In two pilot schools with staffing establishments of 16 and 18 the heads have succeeded in going through the appraisal cycle with all their teachers but have accepted that delegation will be necessary in future. This will provide useful developmental experience for the appraisers, but it will also involve a review of the schools' management structures and a redefinition of responsibilities and job descriptions.

Two-and-a-half years of the project and two-and-a-half terms of pilot work have taught all those involved a number of lessons. These relate principally to training, professional development, the process itself and management.

Before training can begin, it is essential to assess accurately the existing climate of opinion and feeling within the teaching force and at LEA level because this will affect the nature of all that follows. A favourable climate is likely to be one in which there is trust and openness between those involved, a recognition that there are different perspectives which are dependent, among other things, on the contexts within which people work - and a good communications system! If the degree of mutual trust and understanding is less than perfect then awareness-raising must begin by creating it.

There is no point in simply letting people know what is going to happen without setting it in context, clarifying its purpose and indicating the likely outcomes. It must be made clear that appraisal is a two-way process concerned not only with the teacher's work in the classroom and in the school but also with the role of management in facilitating that work through appropriate organisation, adequate resourcing and the provision of support and opportunities for professional development. When you discuss these issues it becomes apparent that, although appraisal begins with teachers, it is also about pupils and about the schools in which they all work.

In all but two of the 19 pilots, 'whole' school training was provided. Cascading may have its virtues but total immersion has its benefits too. There is shared involvement, shared understanding, an opportunity to express doubts and anxieties and to hear the same answers at the same time. It soon became clear that training must lead to practice as soon as possible. The interest engendered is soon dissipated if it is not used and it is unrealistic to believe that in two or three days you can create perfect practitioners. The training packages are no more than starter kits. Getting the car on the road is the next stage and, with sufficient practice, by the end of the first year you should be able to drive unaccompanied. In effect, experience suggests that the whole of the first appraisal is a new process in schools and, assuming an annual cycle, it is likely that it will take two or three years before staff feel wholly comfortable and are able to accept it as part of regular professional practice.

The second lesson was a surprise. The team accepted wholeheartedly the idea that appraisal should 'help individual teachers with their professional development' but interpreted this as meaning only that the process would lead to identified needs being met through in-service training - appropriately resourced! What soon became apparent was that the process itself is developmental. Clarifying your role within the school, carrying out a self-evaluation, being seen at work in the classroom, discussing all this with a senior colleague and setting targets is in itself a valuable and professionally enriching experience. Many of the targets set will refer to professional practice and can be achieved within the school with the support of colleagues. A school's own policy for staff development is likely to be strengthened by appraisal. Externally provided INSET will continue to be important, and in some instances essential, but there is a great deal of expertise in every staffroom. It is in everyone's interests to acknowledge it and to use it.

During the pilot phase it has been possible to fund appraisal Baker days off-site in one of several local conference centres. The facilities are excellent. The main rooms for plenary sessions are spacious and well-appointed and there is accommodation for small discussion groups and workshops. Although there were some comments about 'money that could be better spent', the majority of staff was enthusiastic about the arrangements. They felt that they were 'being treated like professionals', 'being taken seriously'. Outside the familiar school surroundings they were able to concentrate more fully on the training as well as enjoying the experience of being looked after properly. There is some kind of lesson to be learnt from the fact that what would be taken for granted in other spheres of work should be received with such surprised pleasure by teachers.

Similar advantages are to be found in residential courses. Two-and-a-half days' residential training is worth far more than 9 a.m. to 5 p.m. on three consecutive days. It encourages greater involvement, distances people temporarily from other responsibilities and allows for a free flow of professionally useful conversation.

All 'whole school' training has been undertaken by the project team with the help and support of associate trainers. These were teachers, mostly but not exclusively senior staff, who had been members of task groups or had otherwise interested themselves in appraisal and were prepared to be more fully involved. Their role was three-fold: to assist with training, generally as informed group leaders, to be in contact with one of the pilot schools and to collate the evaluation material produced by the staff and to present a report on their pilot work. This was done with the agreement of their heads who recognised it as a useful experience for the teachers concerned and a way of providing senior staff with additional training that would be useful within their own schools. Twenty-two teachers were involved. The group had to be large enough to allow for drop-out and to ensure that no one was over-burdened. In essence, it has worked well. They and their schools have profited from the experience and the team could not have managed training conferences for large secondary schools without their help. There are problems, however. It had originally been intended to give associates the opportunity to deliver training and not to limit them to an exclusively supportive role. In order to do this successfully they would need practice and the reality is that this would have meant either a period of secondment or an unacceptable amount of release from their own schools. Secondment sounds the more attractive alternative but, in fact, it does not provide a complete answer. It needs to be planned well in advance and there is no guarantee that it will be possible to arrange a programme of training that will keep them fully occupied. It seems likely, therefore, that their most useful role is the supportive one, particularly, when the time comes, in their own schools.

Appraisee training was led by Eric Hewton from Sussex University. His book, *The Appraisal Interview* (1988), describes an approach to training that was an inspiration to all who experienced it. The programme included consideration of the appraisal process, concentrating particularly upon classroom observation, target setting, self-evaluation and interview skills. It involved both theory and practice and concluded with real interviews conducted in groups of four and based on the real self-evaluation of one of the group members.

Two elements of the process that are proving to be particularly important are classroom observation and data collection. There is a confusion here which is partly a matter of emphasis and partly a matter of presentation. The ACAS Report provides the emphasis by identifying classroom observation as an essential part of the appraisal process and this is entirely reasonable. Teachers deserve to be seen at work and there is no other way for anyone else to experience the dynamic relationship between teacher and pupil. But is it the only way of evaluating what takes place in the classroom? Is it the only basis for discussion between appraiser and appraisee? If it is, how often should it take place? The conflict between the ideal and the realistic answer has still to be resolved. If it is not, what other ways of evaluation are there? What sort of data other than observation are professionally appropriate?

The belief that appraisal is a developmental process and that teachers should be encouraged to have enough professional self-confidence to discuss their work fully has influenced the way in which 'data collection' has been presented. Restricting the evaluation of a teacher's work to measurable learning outcomes, or even to one observation every one or two years, is to neglect a range of other information about a pupil's progress that is less easy to measure and a number of factors that influence learning but have nothing to do with the teacher, for example, home background, the local community, health, adolescence, attendance. The simple link between the teacher's work and the pupil's success is an appealing one but, like many simplifications, it is by no means the whole story. In the first place, it begs the question of what you mean by success. One child's outstanding achievement is no more than you would expect from another. On what basis then can you measure or describe success?

If you ask teachers if they have made any impact on the pupils with whom they have worked regularly for a whole year few will seriously answer, 'No!' Ask them how they would describe that impact and on what basis they could discuss it and you are beginning to talk about something important in the interaction between teacher and taught. This is the point where presentation has tended to obscure rather than illuminate the issue. Two years ago, teachers were uncomfortable with 'performance indicators', 'outcome indicators', 'principal accountabilities': the language was unfamiliar and smacked, so they said, of industrial approaches to appraisal which were regarded as being wholly inappropriate to education. An attempt to find less threatening alternatives that would at least allow the principle to be discussed led to the use of some rather vaguely defined expressions and produced some surprising reactions. 'Evidence' was dismissed very early because it suggested verdicts and therefore judgments. What happened to self-evaluation? 'Material for discussion' induced fantasies of staggering into an interview with an armful of folders, record books, schemes of work and illustrations of classroom display. 'Data' was a more generally acceptable term though there were those who related this to computer-held information and for them this produced a different and more threatening sort of fantasy. Two-and-a-half years later people are happier to talk about 'learning outcomes' and to consider ways in which they can usefully discuss the link between the teacher's work and the pupil's response.

Three of the basic requirements for successful appraisal are an awareness of the school's aims and objectives, an understanding of the policies designed to meet them and an appreciation of how individual roles complement one another in ensuring that these policies are carried out. Before the appraisal process can begin teachers need a clear job description. Ask them to 'brainstorm' about what they actually do and they will produce an impressive and detailed list of tasks, a daunting agenda for any interview. During training they have been encouraged to go further and to group these tasks into a set of major responsibilities so that discussion may be more usefully focussed. The outcome covers:

- planning and preparation
- classroom teaching

- marking, assessment, reporting
- pastoral work
- contribution to school life
- professional development
- other specific responsibility, for example,
  - head of department
  - curriculum leader
  - year head

There is a wide range of evidence available about all these aspects of teaching and it is worth considering carefully which parts of it are likely to illuminate an appraisal interview and which belong more properly in a different forum, such as a departmental or senior management meeting or a staff working party. For instance, should a particular approach to language teaching be discussed with the teacher concerned or is it an indicator that it is time the school or department reviewed and restated its policy in this area? Is it a matter of support for an individual or a management issue? In the context of this chapter the answer is unimportant. What matters is that appraisal raises such questions and makes it difficult for them to go unanswered.

This is not unconnected with the third important discovery, made early in the project, that appraisal is an aspect of management and not simply an end in itself. It acts as a catalyst, opening up possibilities for action in a variety of areas and, affording as it does opportunities for wide-ranging discussion, it links well with other current initiatives in education. The team recognised also that while a lot of valuable management training was taking place within the borough there was a need to co-ordinate it and to include appraisal within a structured programme of management development and training. In terms of resourcing, it is helpful to see appraisal not as a bolt-on exercise but as part of good management that seeks to capitalise on existing practice. In many schools this is unlikely to include formal observation and an annual interview and, initially, finding time for these may pose problems. What the project has shown is that schools can be endlessly ingenious in finding solutions - but this has been during the pilot phase and supply cover has been available. Ingenuity will not vanish overnight but, if appraisal is to be carried out successfully, offering maximum benefits to the profession, it is important that LMS funding is sufficient to allow heads to manage flexibly and effectively.

A number of practical questions remain. Where should interviews be held and when? How do you guarantee that there will be no interruptions during the school day? How can there be an effective and timely link between a school's appraisal timetable and the LEA INSET programme with its complex arrangements for course planning and bidding for resources? And then there is the whole complex issue of headteacher appraisal. How best do you deal with this in a small, compact authority and in an increasingly competitive climate?

The project has found a number of answers to all these questions, and more, but the most important lesson is that there are few answers that will satisfy everyone. Schools have been provided with the basic elements of an appraisal scheme and have been free to operate it within their own structures. It seems clear that such flexibility is essential if institutions ranging from nursery schools to sixth-form colleges are to manage appraisal successfully.

Pilot work in Croydon has been based on the assumption that appraisal will take place annually, despite the resource implications of this model. It has also assumed that, when the scheme is fully implemented, the cycle will operate over an extended rather than a short period, two terms rather than six weeks. There was general agreement among teachers reporting on their experience that annual frequency and a long cycle would allow a genuine working relationship to develop between appraiser and appraisee and make it more likely that the process would be genuinely developmental. Figure 5.5 indicates the draft proposal for phasing in appraisal over a four-year period.

All those participating in the pilot study were asked to comment on their training and their experience of the appraisal process. This information was collated and discussed at a series of evaluation meetings involving groups of heads, appraisers, appraisees, school appraisal co-ordinators and associate trainers. The exercise produced a mass of information, most of it positive and much of it offering practical advice and suggestions about training and varied approaches to the management of appraisal within the school.

Some remarks were encouraging:

'It was a luxury to have this opportunity for discussion.'

'Appraisal made me more aware of my own role within the whole school development plan. It would have been good to have had it in my first year at the school. I am looking forward to the next one.'

Some were helpful:

'We need more training in self-evaluation and report writing.'

'Success depends on the skill of the appraiser.'

'Cover is essential so that you know your class is taken care of and the interview can run on if necessary.'

Some were illuminating:

'Effective self-evaluation should be the focus of appraisee training.'

Figure 5.5 - Proposed implementation plans (number of schools)

Academic Year

	Secondary	Primary (Incl. nursery)	Special	Advisory Support	Central Support Team
88/9 PILOT Phase 1	7	12 (11 + 1)	-	Advisers/ Coordinators	
89/90 Phase 2	8	10	2		
90/91 Phase 3	8 All	20	2		
91/92 Phase 4	-	31	2 All		
92/93 Phase 5	-	30 All	-		

Implementation plans for the Advisory and Support Services Team have still to be agreed.

Providers

- Team
- Associate trainers
- Sussex University

'There is a danger of concentrating on encouragement and support at the expense of necessary rigour. I would have liked something with more teeth. Perhaps it was because it was the first time round. The second cycle, based on targets, might be more productive.'

Perhaps the final word should he left to a probationer:

'Isn't it great that we can continue the education discussions we had at college.'

Given the right training, enough time and the positive attitudes that have been evident in the pilot schools, there is a fair chance that such informed discussions will indeed take place and that their outcomes will be of genuine benefit both to teachers and their pupils.

Chapter 6

Appraisal and Equal Opportunities

Meryl Thompson

When women manage schools children's academic achievement is greater, teachers have higher morale and parents respond to the school more favourably. These conclusions from American research (Shakeshaft 1989) contrast tellingly with the evidence that in Britain women's promotion prospects for senior management posts have deteriorated in the last 20 years. This evidence of women's leadership abilities contrasts even more dramatically with the common assumption in Britain that qualities such as detachment and toughness, usually attributed to men, are essential leadership characteristics. The reason for these frequent contrasts between the empirical evidence and our personal assumptions, widely-held social generalisations and some theoretical hypotheses is that human beings largely act, not on the basis of objective facts or reasonable evidence, but on a series of unexamined assumptions and more or less sophisticated generalisations. Rather than make critical judgments, we pre-judge. We thoughtlessly and habitually use generalisations, including racial and sexual stereotypes, rather than examine each situation afresh. We tend to act emotionally rather than rationally. We condone behaviour in people we like, or who are like us, that we condemn in others. We make scapegoats. We project on to others behavioural characteristics we dislike in ourselves. Admittedly, some people show a greater degree of objectivity, more flexibility to modify their opinions and are less inclined to jump to conclusions than others, but the predisposition remains. Generalisations after all also help us to order and categorise our experience. In appraisal, where teachers are asked to make a series of wide-ranging professional judgments, this psychological and cognitive tendency will be the permanent backcloth.

Early in the debate about the introduction of appraisal for teachers it was argued that an open and formal appraisal scheme would be preferable to the present informal and covert way decisions concerning teachers' careers are made. Inherent in this argument is the assumption that appraisal, by providing a basis of objective criteria and a systematic procedure for professional development and career planning, would counter subjectivity and partiality and contribute to achieving equal opportunities in the widest sense. As the National Steering Group's Report (1989) stated, 'appraisal must operate and be seen to operate, fairly and equitably for all teachers' and 'should be used positively to promote equal opportunities by encouraging all teachers to fulfil their potential.' Equal opportunities issues are therefore central to implementing appraisal. Certainly, appraisal will lose credibility with sections of the profession if they perceive structural prejudices and discrimination unaddressed and unaltered.

It became evident during the co-ordination conferences organised by the National Development Centre that the variable but undeveloped level of awareness of equal opportunities issues is one of the many deficiencies in educational management which appraisal tends to highlight. Some of the pilot projects had intentionally used both a male and female presenter to disseminate information and raise awareness and had deliberately selected trainers to ensure gender balance and to include teachers with varying responsibilities to counteract the hierarchical structure appraisers represent, but there was no detailed practical experience of how issues relating to gender or race should be incorporated into appraisal schemes. This was somewhat redressed by the recommendations of a NDC working group which were largely incorporated into the NSG Report. The NSG recommended that the circular should stress the need for appraisers to be aware of their legal responsibilities not to discriminate on grounds of sex, race or marital status and of the danger of stereotyped expectations which result in a biased approach when conducting appraisal. However, exactly how appraisal policies and procedures can address the existing inequalities in professional development and career opportunities for teachers arising from discrimination and stereotyping remains to be considered.

The legislation which outlaws discrimination on the grounds of race, ethnic origins, gender and marital status will apply to appraisal procedures because appraisal contributes to identifying staff development and training needs. Direct or indirect sex discrimination is unlawful under the Sex Discrimination Act 1975 in employment and includes discrimination in opportunities for promotion, transfer, training and education. Direct sex discrimination occurs when one person is treated less favourably on the grounds of sex than a person of the other sex is or would be treated. Indirect sex discrimination occurs when a requirement or condition is applied equally to men and women but has the practical effect of disadvantaging a considerably higher proportion of one sex than the other. The 1976 Race Relations Act makes direct or indirect discrimination on the grounds of a person's colour, race, nationality or ethnic origins similarly unlawful.

Therefore, as the NSG Report and the Equal Opportunities Commission recommend, each appraisal scheme should be monitored to assess how it works in practice. This will mean examining the outcomes of the professional targets for development and training identified by appraisal to see if there is an imbalance between sexes or ethnic groups which suggests that unlawful direct or indirect discrimination is occurring. If so, the cause must be identified to ensure that it is not discriminatory. However, the LEA's responsibility does not stop there, for if an employee unlawfully discriminates in the course of employment both employee and employer are responsible whether or not the employer knows or approves of the action, unless the employer has taken all reasonable steps to prevent discrimination. Therefore, LEAs must take positive action to prevent appraisers from practising discrimination by, for example, including unbiased managerial practice in the criteria for appraising appraisers and the provision of equal opportunities for all the staff in the criteria for appraising headteachers and by ensuring that any assessment criteria used in appraisal are not discriminatory. What is also clear is that LEAs must provide appropriate advice on equal opportunities directly to schools and in appraisal training. Knowledge of the legislation alone will not alter the existing management structures and structural prejudices which may cause discrimination and into which appraisal will be incorporated, and the introduction of appraisal requires that these are more fully understood.

Although women outnumber men in the teaching profession they are seriously under-represented in senior positions. In 1985, one in ten male teachers was a headteacher. For women the figure was one in 25. In the secondary sector women formed 55 per cent of the teaching force, but only 31 per cent of those on scale 3 or above, compared to 58 per cent of men. The latest DES returns for the primary sector in England show the same pattern with women disproportionately placed in posts of lower or no responsibility. Women formed 79.9 per cent of the full-time and 87 per cent of the part-time teaching force and of these, 76.7 per cent and 96.1 per cent respectively were on Scales 1 and 2, compared to 35 per cent of male full-time teachers. Of the male full-time teachers only 9 per cent had no responsibility, compared to 32 per cent of the women. At the other end of the scale, 32 per cent of men were headteachers and 21 per cent deputy headteachers, compared with 7.5 per cent and 8.5 per cent respectively for women. Furthermore, even these statistics conceal the effect of including nursery and separate infant schools, where almost all teachers are women. In 1987 69.4 per cent of infant/junior headships and 79.6 per cent of junior headships were held by men, although they made up only 25 per cent and 34 per cent of the teachers in such schools.

Men's career chances are therefore substantially better than women's. As the EOC said, this is a wastage of skill and talent and a matter of concern to everyone involved with the teaching profession, because it may indicate a pattern of under-achievement by women in an area of employment in which there is a well-established tradition of female participation. The causal factors are difficult to identify. An AMMA survey found that although only slightly fewer women described themselves as interested in progressing through the career structure, 57 per cent of men compared to 34 per cent of women were heads, deputy heads or heads of departments. The reason seemed to be that 44 per cent of women teachers, compared with only 14 per cent of men teachers, had had a break in service lasting a year or more. Moreover, for men the breaks were usually for further study, training or research - activities which could improve promotion prospects. Women teachers were more likely to have made an enforced sideways move because of a change in the husband's job.

However, there is also extensive evidence that the present situation is in part due to a sex-differentiated management response to women's and men's development needs which determines what type of training and experience is offered to women and men teachers. For example, one teacher described how men on scale 3 were 'approached by the head to go on management courses - none of the female members of staff was encouraged or even asked to think about it. So I suppose that he did not think that the married women on the staff were interested in promotion' (Al-Khalifa, 1989). This is consistent with a survey of the insurance industry where a significant percentage of managers believed women were not interested in a career, while an overwhelming majority of the women considered career advancement a high priority for job satisfaction (Bargh, 1988). In the Civil Service women receive performance ratings as good as men, but lower promotability ratings. Women, it seems, are being excluded from promotion because of under-assessment by their line managers, who may act on unjustified assumptions quite sub-consciously and attribute to all women attitudes and opinions which may not be held by the woman being appraised. The existence of such stereotyping is supported by research into women teachers' actual experience of discrimination. Women are commonly questioned in interviews, even by headteachers, on child care arrangements and domestic responsibilities. It is assumed that it is their work which will suffer because women must automatically undertake these responsibilities.

It is obvious that the standard pattern in teaching will be a male manager appraising a female. Even more frequently a white manager will be appraising a black teacher. The danger is that certain assumptions, attitudes and stereotypes which can shape the way an individual's potential is perceived could pervade the appraisal process. It is essential that appraisal training challenges rather than reinforces these attitudes. The common sex stereotypes can be categorised neatly. Prestigious qualities such as reason, objectivity, leadership, independence and authority have been attributed to men, while women have been allocated stigmatised qualities such as emotion, irrationality, passivity and dependence. Al-Khalifa quotes an LEA officer explaining to a woman deputy headteacher who had failed to gain a headship, 'It's a tough situation, awkward governors, a lot to be done. Needs a man; he won't get so involved.' She also argues that recent developments in management theory, which stress school organisational problems as technical problems amenable to rational problem-solving, emphasise characteristics such as 'analytical detachment' and 'hard-nosed toughness' that are commonly seen as 'masculine'. Leadership characteristics are thus seen to correspond to the socially determined masculine sex-role.

Conversely, when women display just these characteristics their ambition and 'hardness' are seen as unnatural and unfeminine and result in pejorative comments. For there are also stereotyped perceptions of the appropriate and inappropriate behaviour and demeanours of each sex. The common conception of femininity involves modesty, deference (to the male), non-aggressiveness and being agreeable. As Spender (1989) says, 'In a society which assumes the politeness and deference of women towards men as the norm women who do not defer to men are often judged by men and women as socially unacceptable.' Men may prefer to promote women who are 'passive and non-threatening or at least capable of appearing so' (Shakeshaft, 1989). Cunnison (1989) argues that much male humour is designed to undermine women in authority by reminding women of their sexuality and by restating sexual and domestic stereotypes thus implicitly suggesting their administrative incompetence. Women can be deterred from ever assuming posts of responsibility over others and may still be discouraged from promotion by a widely-held assumption that their health and that of their families will suffer. There also remains a deeply-seated belief that men have more right to promotion because they are the main breadwinners.

Women's attitudes also contribute to the generalised supposition that management responsibilities at whatever level are more appropriately undertaken by men. Women are described and sometimes describe themselves as too diffident, poor at job interviews and playing safe in terms of the posts for which they apply. They lack confidence in their competence to teach science because it is perceived as 'masculine' and believe that their male colleagues can compensate for their own limited technical knowledge. Their stereotypes include the perception that male headteachers will inevitably be authoritarian, unbending and intolerant. Some women teachers also seem to credit men with higher standards and clearer vision, which may affect their ability to contribute professionally to their self-evaluation and to the professional dialogue of appraisal. Unexamined sexual stereotyping in the assumptions of appraisers and in the influence they have on the way women appraisees perceive and project themselves and their position can therefore influence appraisal. Appraisers and appraisees must be made aware of how sexual stereotyping can be part of our generally shared perceptions and that it can affect self-evaluation and self-presentation.

Male appraisers must be careful to estimate confident, autonomous and assertive (possibly young) women by the same standards as men. Men in general talk more and interrupt more in mixed-sex contexts. Women who consistently and successfully control verbal interaction are frequently criticised by men and are likely to be regarded as 'bitchy', domineering or aggressive. To allow a woman in an appraisal interview 80 per cent of the time to express her views and talk of her priorities may be very difficult for many men. Psychologically, the attempt may not work in the woman's favour - witness the disgruntled reaction of boys where a deliberate attempt had been made to give an equal time to talk for girls (Spender, 1989). Women may need to learn to state clearly what they want from appraisal and discuss realistic timetables and programmes of action for achieving this because, 'too often women assume that if they have had a good performance review then the manager will automatically put them forward for promotion. In reality this is rarely the case' (Bargh, 1988). Women also tend to get less negative feedback, either through chivalry or a fear that women will burst into tears (and the man be discomfited in handling it). Thus they are frequently denied constructive criticism that could improve their performance. Therefore, both men and women need training in giving and receiving feedback constructively.

One stereotype which may particularly influence appraisal is the low status typically ascribed to infant and early years teaching, which is disparaged as an extension of mothering and child care. As one teacher commented, 'Senior Management of combined J/I schools is predominantly male. Female attributes and their commitment to early school education is often overlooked and/or held in low regard' (Al-Khalifa, 1987). Other stereotyped assumptions could influence the assessment of classroom management styles. Women teachers who establish discipline through developing relationships and reasoning with pupils rather than dictating to them are taken less seriously than 'hard teachers'.

It should be evident, therefore, that gender stereotypes do need to be considered in appraisal training if appraisal is to be fair and equitable and promote equal opportunities, but it may not be enough. For example, to make allowances for women's diffidence, male appraisers may press on women teachers managerial responsibilities and ambitions which women believe are genuinely inappropriate for them, considering their priorities and values. Men may be unable to appreciate this and misinterpret their reluctance to accept responsibility. This could reinforce the stereotype when what may be involved here are two differing value systems. This possibility is supported by evidence that male and female attitudes to work differ greatly. Comparative studies of men and women in 65 occupations found that most men work for money and career advancement. Men are always looking up the ladder for the main chance whereas women seek job satisfaction, a good working atmosphere and flexibility to fit family life into their careers. They emphasise doing a thorough job and doing the job well. Women work for self-fulfilment, for social relationships and like to feel they are making a contribution and are valued by colleagues. Research suggests that these attitudes are shared by teachers too. Women teachers value classroom teaching and put it as a priority. For them teaching and not management is 'real work'. They are more hesitant about career moves unless they have assessed their readiness. They weigh all the factors they feel impinge on their career and professional development, including their classroom strengths and weaknesses, their commitments outside work, and the obligations these present in maintaining relationships and meeting family needs. In comparison, men teachers show little interest in this kind of self-evaluation, do not mention their home situation and see their future essentially in terms of promotion moves.

This coincides with a major American survey which suggests that the contrast in male and female attitudes is more radically different than those who merely wish to clear away stereotypes have appreciated. In *In a Different Voice*, Gilligan (1982) describes two different value systems, two modes of thinking about relationships by men and women. In itself this is not new. Historically, women have been regarded as intellectually and morally more feeble than men. Freud thought women 'showed less sense of justice and were more often influenced in their judgements by feelings of affection or hostility.' Gilligan (1982) provides a different evaluation. For boys and men, separation and individuation are critically tied to their gender identity since separation from the mother is essential for the development of masculinity. For girls and women they are not. Male gender identity is threatened by intimacy while female gender identity is threatened by separation. Males tend to have difficulty with relationships while females have problems with individuation. This results in two different moral ideologies. Men emphasise rights and women responsibilities since separation can only be justified by an ethic of rights and attachment is supported by an ethic of care. The morality of rights is predicated on equality and centred on the understanding of fairness, that of responsibility relies on the concept of equity and the recognition of differences in need. Girls emerge with a basis for empathy built into their primary definition of self in a way that boys do not. Women, it is argued, have a stronger basis for experiencing as their own another's needs and feelings. Women stress co-operation and collaboration, men autonomy and individuality.

Many aspects of appraisal emphasise contributing to the development of others, whether colleagues or students, and this suggests that male values and modes of behaviour are not the most appropriate models. A value system of responsibilities and care seems more appropriate to appraisal than one of rights and individuality. Also, the American research already quoted indicates that women administrators spend more time with people, care more about individual differences, motivate more and their staff have more shared professional goals. Women administrators demonstrate a more democratic and participatory management style, exhibit greater knowledge of teaching methods and techniques and create a school climate more conducive to learning (Shakeshaft, 1989). Women are also considered 'better listeners' and listening skills are regarded as essential in appraisal. The skill is not only to let the appraisee contribute but to pick up nuances and to detect the underlying assumptions, attitudes and emotions that give the whole picture. It requires both empathy and a concern for others. Men may lack these skills because they are too used to dominating meetings and putting their own arguments. Certainly, women do not believe men are good listeners and often feel that men only take seriously ideas presented by men. In appraisal, listening is given a role as complex as talking, although in social life it is devalued in mixed-sex conversation and associated with passivity (Spender, 1985). Conventional male styles of verbal interaction will not dominate in appraisal and because this disturbs the balance of power between the sexes may add to the discomfort of interviews with the opposite sex.

In other ways, too, women teachers' values, their attitude to being a good teacher and their tendency to be more introspective and hesitant about their professional strengths and weaknesses may be a more appropriate starting point for appraisal. For appraisal is not directly and immediately about promotion, although the qualities and strengths it enhances and develops should not be irrelevant to the qualities and strengths required by teachers with managerial responsibilities. It is about continuous and systematic development as a professional. This makes appraisal relevant for all teachers at whatever stage of their careers. It relates appraisal to improving the quality of learning experiences for children and simultaneously promoting job satisfaction and professional pride and autonomy in teachers. Ironically, male weaknesses, in failing to evaluate the intrinsic quality of the job they are doing, in having too much uncritical confidence in their own worth and promotability and in valuing where they are going more than the fulfilment to be gained from making a contribution here and now, may make this essential formative and developmental element of appraisal less satisfying and less convincing for them. There are interesting parallels with boys' and girls' attitudes to records of achievement where there is evidence that girls understand the purpose of the formative processes better than boys. The National Steering Committee concluded that girls 'tend to be more forthcoming and skilled in discussion and value the opportunity for one to one contact with their teachers. On the other hand boys tend to have a keener sense of the external audience for the records of achievement rather than relationships.'

However, if by and large men are to be the appraisers then ensuring male commitment to formative appraisal and to the intrinsic and personal elements of professional development must be an essential part of appraisal training. Otherwise male appraisers may find women's attitudes to work deficient because they regard career-centred values as the measure of seriousness and interest in work. If commitment to appraisal for professional development remains superficial and only thinly conceals the expectation that appraisal is about promotion for those with the right qualities - masculine ones - women's likely expectations for appraisal will be severely disappointed. Men in managerial positions could even have their power reinforced. Formative appraisal requires openness and critical self-evaluation, but power, it is argued, often lies with those who do not disclose their vulnerabilities and who abstain from self-revelation and withhold personal information. Remaining aloof while someone else discloses personal information facilitates dominance. If formative appraisal were to reinforce this dominance and leave women more vulnerable, women would have to think carefully about its consequences.

Moreover, if the developmental purpose of appraisal is not fully understood and implemented, the consequences will be dysfunctional. Appraisal would not then contribute to improving professional dialogue or to a better understanding and appreciation of the skills of teaching or to sharing what we learn to improve the teaching and learning environment of the school. It would not help teachers fulfil their potential. Appraisal as conceived by the pilot projects and the NSG, however, will focus on reflection, self-evaluation, professional development and improving teaching and learning and not only on promotion. It is likely to change the focus of teaching to one that is more congenial to women. As managerial responsibilities begin to include responsibility for appraisal - and thus the responsibility to encourage the skills of teaching analysis and classroom observation and obligations to the development of professional colleagues - managerial roles will also be more in line with women's values. The role of headteacher as an educational leader will be more attractive to women than the role of headteacher as administrator.

As Al-Khalifa (1989) points out, knowledge and experience of such gender-linked issues are not normally part of the required preparation for management and staff development is generally conceptualised as gender-neutral. But, if we are to ensure fair and unbiased appraisals, sexual stereotypes and our common assumptions concerning women's place in society must be replaced by a more objective and more individualised assessment of their relative professional strengths and weaknesses. The same considerations apply in other areas of stereotyping and prejudice, such as the assessments made of teachers from ethnic minorities and in age discrimination.

The under-representation of teachers from ethnic minority groups is another major concern to all those in education and from January 1990 returns must be made on the ethnic origins of teachers. The aim is to provide data to support fair and equal employment opportunities and additional details of sex, age, phase, specialism and form of employment will be collected by the DES. However, in 1988 a survey of eight LEAs found that only two per cent of teachers was black and evidence showed that they were disproportionately on the lower salary scales. It concluded that teachers from ethnic minorities do not enjoy the same career progression as white teachers and headteachers do not encourage them to apply for vacancies within the school in the same way as white teachers. An ILEA survey in 1987 found that, ' black teachers were severely and negatively affected during reorganisation and amalgamations of schools when demotions were more likely for black teachers than promotions or holding on to their substantive posts.'

In order to counteract structural prejudices and discrimination, appraisal training will similarly need to acknowledge the context in which ethnic minority teachers find themselves - a context which is rarely openly discussed. Teachers from ethnic minorities will be well aware of racial prejudice and stereotypes, of racial attacks on minority groups, of racist graffiti, and they may be personally affected by the publicity given to incidents such as the boycott of the Dewsbury School by white parents and the bias against those with non-British names built into the computer program of St George's Medical School. These teachers may even have experienced racist remarks from their own teachers and racist attitudes restricting their own educational achievement by an underestimate of their potential. Grievances on grounds of racial harassment are not unknown in teaching, although there is little firm evidence of their extent. There is also the 'insidious, unconscious racism of white teachers who fail to recognise that their black colleagues may feel ill at ease in a mainly white staff room or may need some support to cope with harassment they suffer outside school' (AMMA, 1988). However, this social context and the way it influences relationships with colleagues and their perceptions is not always understood in teaching.

Only now are black teachers' experiences and perspectives of schools and their management finding a wider audience. These experiences include having their identity, as black persons and members of minority groups, ignored, particularly as students, yet finding their working lives dominated by issues to do with race. Assumptions are made that black teachers can speak for all the local black community even if they personally know little about other ethnic groups and cultures. They are used as convenient intermediaries to pass on messages or discuss difficult issues with black colleagues and are expected to fill disciplinary and pastoral roles in delicate situations, often being asked to intervene on behalf of the school rather than in the interests of the black pupils and parents. As one black teacher said, 'A school can deflect allegations of racism by using its black staff to deal with situations of tension, and even by citing their existence as proof of its commitment to challenging racism' (Bangar and McDermott, 1989; McKellar, 1989).

It is frequently assumed that black teachers will work only or largely with ethnic minority children. A revealing example of this pervasive attitude occurs in a supposedly exemplary appraisal interview. A young teacher is asked, 'Have there been any disappointments during the year?' and responds with, 'Not really apart from the fact that I still don't have my own class. I think that people see me as some sort of superior classroom helper. I'm not. I'm a fully qualified teacher, but just because I can speak Panjabi I have to stay ...' The explanatory comment acknowledges this is an important and valid point and a highly emotional issue which a teacher would quite legitimately want to make sure was raised during the appraisal interview. The advice to the appraiser is that one cannot allow the interview to be side-tracked from the agreed agenda because the headteacher has to deploy the staff to meet the children's needs (Rhodes, 1988). Thus the issues of equal opportunities, structural prejudice and personal identity are ignored.

Teachers from ethnic minorities have the same right to opportunities for complete professional development from appraisal and the same right to be regarded as individuals, which means that their specific needs and experience as a part of a minority group cannot be ignored. School management must become aware of how it may be involving these teachers unreasonably. Fair and equal treatment means varying and sensitive treatment. It requires understanding, confidence and maturity in the appraiser which may not be acquired unless the introductory materials and appraisal training emphasise the significance of these issues and help appraisers to develop the necessary understanding and skills.

It is perhaps only now being recognised that prejudices that limit equality of opportunity extend to stereotyped assumptions about what is appropriate and beneficial at varying ages. Potentially this is sexual discrimination and the EOC recommends that on these grounds age limits for access to training and promotion should be questioned. However, on all grounds for equality, appraisal training should ensure that it is not assumed that in-service training (with its related expenses) is inappropriate for those near retirement or that teachers over 50 will prefer premature retirement to challenges in the classroom and increased responsibilities. In fact, the AMMA survey found 70 per cent of the 40-49 age group and 48 per cent of the over-50s still interested in progressing in their career.

There are also important factors which are relevant to inter-personal skills training. Although individuals vary, it is generally more difficult to adapt one's teaching styles if these are the product of some 30 years' experience. All change brings with it a sense of becoming de-skilled and demoralised and a certain percentage of fear. Appraisers should be particularly careful not to damage the sense of self-worth and the lifetime achievement of those very near the end of their teaching career and to allow for the psychological process of adapting to retirement. Appraisal by younger teachers may threaten the sense of dignity of older teachers. Mores, courtesies and vocabularies do change but nothing in appraisal should precipitate the decision of an experienced but perhaps demoralised professional to leave teaching. Many teachers, particularly men, who tend to have greater expectations of promotion, must come to terms with disappointment as they age. Sometimes male anger and resentment may be deflected on to women, especially those on their way up. As appraisers, women may have to learn to manage this and turn it into something positive. Certainly, to achieve the trust and confidence of these experienced classroom teachers will require considerable professional and personal skills.

It should now be obvious that issues of equal opportunities must be integrated at every stage of implementing appraisal. LEAs have been asked to set the climate for appraisal and to raise awareness. In particular, positive reassurances should be given at this stage that equal opportunities will be respected. Each LEA should make it clear that the existence of racial and sexual harassment is a legitimate area of concern. Sexual harassment is possibly the most difficult area of inter-personal relationships in appraisal. It has been defined by the NUT as 'any uninvited, unreciprocated and unwelcome physical contact, comment, suggestion, joke or attention which is offensive to the person involved and causes that person to feel threatened, humiliated, patronised or embarrassed.' It may create a threatening and intimidating working environment, adversely affect job performance and, in extreme cases, may cause a person to seek to leave the school. Sexual harassment is widespread with surveys all showing a high proportion of women reporting unwanted attentions from men.

In the only specific survey of women secondary teachers 65 per cent of the 246 respondents had experienced sexual harassment, predominantly from male colleagues (Addison and Al-Khalifa, 1988). The most common experience, of being eyed up and down or of suggestive looks at parts of the body, was recorded by two in five of the respondents. Regular sexual jokes and innuendo were reported almost as often. More than one in five of the women teachers had experienced 'touching, brushing against, patting, pinching or grabbing.' Even more seriously one in ten reported a direct sexual proposition and six reported forcible sexual aggression from male colleagues. For appraisal, the most serious aspect is likely to be the pervasiveness of suggestive looks and sexual innuendo. Classroom observation could become a degrading and humiliating experience for women teachers, resulting in considerable modifications to manner, behaviour and dress, and imposing a high degree of unnaturalness in order to avoid being the object of unwanted sexual attention in a professional teaching environment. Women will be unable to continue the avoidance tactics reported by a third of the respondents in the survey. Sexual remarks, jokes and innuendo can be part of 'staffroom banter' and to complain can be regarded as churlish. Like black people complaining of racism, women are often told that they are imagining that actions are suggestive or lascivious. Yet sexual jokes and generally making fun of women constantly draw attention back to a woman's sex and femininity. Subtly, this implies that women are less competent and less committed to their job and undermines their authority.

If appraisal is to be as positive and supportive for women as for men these issues will have to be confronted to end what one teacher in the survey described as 'fighting two battles - the things you want to achieve professionally and how to cope with men, because in their eyes you are a woman and not a teacher.' Women teachers must feel confident that they will not have to tolerate the danger of behaviour which may be bearable in the semi-social context of the staffroom but which impairs and diminishes the professional interaction essential in appraisal. It would also be unendurable for women teachers who have experienced 'touching up' were the appraiser the perpetrator. Close proximity in a private interviewing room would bring the fear of humiliation and negate a woman teacher's ability to evaluate her professional contribution. However, sexual harassment is often unreported because it causes high levels of anxiety and stress. Women find it difficult to talk about. In the Birmingham survey 74 per cent of the women did not complain at all, largely because they believed the reaction would be negative and that what had happened would not be regarded as serious enough; when they did complain 31 per cent reported that no action was taken and where action was taken 71 per cent was not satisfied with the outcome.

The introduction of appraisal requires an open recognition that sexual harassment is properly regarded as a disciplinary misdemeanour which will tangibly affect career prospects if a managerial position is exploited. LEAs must take particular care to deal effectively with all complaints of harassment and, most importantly, not assume that they are made by women who are over sensitive. Awareness-raising materials, training courses for appraisers, and management courses should raise the issue so that before the introduction of appraisal each school examines whether its ethos and climate allows all its teachers the same personal respect. It should be widely acknowledged during awareness raising that the selection of an appraiser would be reconsidered sensitively if sexual or racial harassment was a factor.

This first stage of introducing appraisal should also include an assessment of the awareness of equal opportunities issues within the LEA. The legal basis for direct and indirect discrimination and the NSG recommendation on the dangers of stereotyping and bias should be widely disseminated and referred to in both the preliminary literature and the training programmes. The training programme should incorporate the factual information on the position of women and ethnic minority teachers in the profession and disseminate relevant research. Some authorities may wish to disseminate their own equal opportunities policies and some schools may consider integrating gender and race issues raised by appraisal with issues related to the curriculum and in line with their own school policies. The selection of trainers should also ensure the best possible balance of gender and ethnic groupings, especially where the LEA decides to train its own trainers. A balance here between age, sex, ethnic grouping and position in the teaching hierarchy can do a great deal to overcome the imbalance in a typical school's management structure and contribute to creating the right climate for emphasising equal opportunities in appraisal.

The principle that appraisers must guard against anything that distorts reality, favourably or unfavourably, is embodied in all appraisal schemes and so sexual and racial stereotypes, and the unexamined prejudices and assumptions which are often part of our behaviour patterns must be considered and explained in appraisal training. For example, performance or behaviour which would be overlooked or condoned in one sex must not be noted as significant in the other. Appraisees, too, need to understand the significance of stereotyping in their inter-personal transactions and in self-evaluation and self-presentation. Undoubtedly this will be one of the more difficult areas of training since it requires not only attitudinal changes but the development of self-critical skills. The training must be experiential and allow teachers the chance to recognise when they are using unexamined assumptions and stereotypes. Video-taped situations and paired observation can help to alert teachers to what not to do. In skills such as handling potential conflict it is likely that repeated practice, coaching and remedial training will be appropriate. For some people this aspect of appraisal training will not be comfortable and schools and LEAs should give serious consideration to the need for counselling both during training and to protect those who feel unfairly treated because of intended or unintended stereotyping when appraisal is implemented.

Equal opportunities should also be part of the criteria for assessing the school and the educational system. The extent to which the LEA or the school is delivering equal opportunities can be measured by the nature of the staffing structure, the allocation of incentive allowances and the outcomes of appraisal. To be effective, this requires efficient monitoring of where both ethnic minority group teachers and women teachers are in the educational system relative to their experience and qualifications.

LEAs will also have to consider how well their own structures reflect a concern for equal opportunities issues. Men make up 75.5 per cent of the total advisers but women make up 40 per cent of the primary advisers and only 17.5 per cent of the secondary ones (Stillman and Grant, 1989). It is likely that similar sexual and racial stereotypes and similar prejudices are prevalent within LEA management. The need to update and enhance the skills of LEA advisers and officers is now widely recognised and should include equal opportunities issues, particularly in the light of the introduction of appraisal. Researchers, too, can contribute by always looking for possible differences in male and female teachers' experiences, skills and attitudes in teaching. Age and membership of an ethnic minority group should be regarded as possibly significant variables wherever relevant. In this way we can improve the evidential base, against which we can test our assumptions.

However, all this will be irrelevant if sensitive and practical steps are not taken genuinely to face gender and race issues in schools. Situations where graffiti is referred to in assembly because of the damage to property rather than for its racist nature and where sexual harassment by students is regarded as a disciplinary failure in the teacher rather than an issue for the school, cannot co-exist with a climate that ensures a fair appraisal for all teachers. Neither can we ignore the influence practical problems, such as lack of child-care facilities, have on women's ability to concentrate on their own professional development through INSET. The approach to equal opportunities must be consistent and unvarying or else the intent that appraisal should be used positively to promote equal opportunities will lose its credibility.

It is difficult to see how writers on appraisal can describe it as a fairer and more up-to-date basis for making professional judgments and yet, as so many do, ignore equal opportunities issues entirely. The NSG has quite properly placed fair and equitable treatment of all teachers at the centre of the appraisal process and has stated categorically that appraisal should be used positively *to promote equal opportunities* by encouraging all teachers to fulfil their potential. It has recognised that stereotyping and the bias that arises from both prejudice and partiality are barriers to fairness and equity. The stark fact is that we can make no attempt at an objective assessment without consciously and explicitly considering the effect our unexamined assumptions and our own value system have on the process and without testing our assumptions against behavioural and other evidence. This applies in every appraisal. The issues raised by gender, race and age are, however, deeply embedded in both our subconscious and our emotive ways of thinking. They must be faced directly and specifically. The introduction of appraisal moves equal opportunities issues to the pivotal point in awareness raising and training and makes this the greatest challenge and the greatest opportunity for radical change in the structure and the values of the teaching profession.

Chapter 7

Teacher Appraisal - the Cumbria Experience

Terry Buckler

In July 1984 the Cumbria Education Authority set up a working party to look into school evaluation and individual staff appraisal and development. This was largely in response to *Teaching Quality*, the paper issued by the Department of Education and Science in March 1983. The elected members agreed that the working party should include representatives of both major political groups on the County Council, although it is worth noting that at the time the Labour group had a working majority. The recognised teachers' associations each had two places and the director of education invited certain officers, inspectors/advisers and headteachers to take part. In order to give a clear view as to why the teachers' associations were able to co-operate with the development of teacher appraisal in the county and why the members of those associations supported the eventual scheme, it is necessary to examine the chronological events leading to the agreed policy and then to look at the operation of that policy.

The terms of reference of the working party were, 'to examine the need for schools' self-evaluation, staff development and appraisal.' The chair of the staffing sub-committee of the education committee also chaired the working party: it met regularly and at an early stage determined to investigate the value of some system of 'whole school' review combined with an approach to the professional development of teachers. In addition, it recognised the particular challenges and importance of arriving at an appropriate scheme for *all* schools, including the small primary schools: some 70 schools had two or fewer staff, including the head.

After considerable research into developments in other authorities in the United Kingdom, into approaches adopted in Canada and examples of good practice in Cumbria's own schools, it was decided to run small pilot studies into both 'whole school' review and professional development, based on a career review approach. The latter had shown the working party the need to determine the place of assessment in such a review. After wide-ranging debate, it was agreed unanimously to develop this mini-pilot as a professional development model, to avoid any reference to assessment and, instead, to use the approach to appraise the role of individual staff. The two strands - 'whole school' review and career development - of what was to become known as the Cumbria scheme were given trials separately in volunteer schools. Even at this early stage the teachers' associations' representatives ensured that both schools and individual staff were not pressurised into taking part and that they had a full opportunity to discuss the situation.

The 'whole school' review approach was eventually based upon GRIDS - 'Guidelines for the Review and Internal Development of Schools' - which had been pioneered by the Schools Council. Recognising the particular problems facing small primary schools, it was agreed that a group of such schools should work together to determine whether or not there were modifications that could be made to GRIDS to make it an appropriate tool to use in such schools. The fact that GRIDS is a most 'democratic' approach to review and is 'owned' by the staff as a whole commended it to the working party and particularly to the teachers' associations' representatives. It was interesting that staff in the trial schools, particularly the small primary schools, did not see the need for the high level of confidentiality involved but, rather, indicated the importance of professional trust and honesty between all involved.

'Individual career development' approaches had not been widely researched in this country and it was not possible to take a nationally recognised scheme and adapt and develop it for use in Cumbria. The working party therefore took as a base a model used in one of the county's comprehensive schools and developed it for trial on a wider basis. The thrust of the scheme depended on a 'career interview' between the head of the school and an individual member of staff and then built on structured self-evaluation to provide a foundation for the discussion.

These early stages in developing a scheme were made possible by Local Authority funding. This meant that time was available, particularly in the small schools, and showed the commitment of both officers and elected members. It was particularly obvious from the feedback that the 'whole school' review would provide a most appropriate base for looking at the development needs of an individual teacher. In addition, it was evident that, in order to inform the career development discussion, more information was essential, in particular about the teaching situation. The working party now looked at how to bring together the different elements of the pilot study and how to incorporate the findings in a coherent policy, an integral part of which was the appraisal of teachers.

It was agreed that appraisal of a teacher's job should take place only in the context of an internal self-review by the school and that the review should be clearly 'owned' by staff. The authority would have no access to the results of such a review and thus the necessary openness and professional trust would be easier to develop. As to the professional development or appraisal stage, this would need to be properly funded both in terms of time and money.

The working party was now in a position to work out the detail of a further policy paper to put to the education committee. It embodied the above principles and fleshed out the time and finance needed to complete the exercise, including preparation, training provision, clerical support, supply cover arrangements and the actual processes of review and appraisal. Cost of appraisal varies according to purpose and method but formative, developmental appraisal, which is geared to enhancing the whole quality of the learning process through the encouragement of effective teaching, must be funded at an appropriate level to ensure that it is both valued and valuable.

It had become obvious from the mini-pilot that, if individual teacher appraisal were to work, it had to be based upon the best possible information and had to include some sort of observation of a teacher's job. The whole idea of 'classroom observation' was and is a sensitive issue for many teachers and, in the view of the teachers' associations in Cumbria, is a term which sends out the wrong message. Our aim was to develop a scheme in which teachers had complete trust - and observation suggested something akin to student teaching practice or something undertaken during inspections. The working party agreed on 'teaching analysis' to cover this essential area of the process, with the nature of such analysis being negotiated between appraisee and appraiser. Individual job specifications would be required so that both parties would be clear about the job being appraised.

Perhaps the most important statement agreed by all members of the working party related to finance: the education committee was recommended to adopt the scheme in principle, but not to implement it until sufficient funding could be assured. The education committee unanimously agreed to all the proposals and the teachers' associations all agreed the policy statement as approved by the committee. The role of the associations in the working party had been significant and the level of support from elected members of all political parties for the developmental approaches set out in the policy convinced the representatives of those associations of the value of continuing the work. It was now October 1985: Cumbria had an agreed policy on teacher appraisal but no funding to develop it further.

In an attempt to make progress, representatives of the Authority, including elected members, officers, and the author (representing the teachers' associations), visited the Department of Education and Science. Again, the importance of the associations had been recognised and valued. The purpose of the visit was to try to persuade the DES to provide funding for a bigger pilot than had been possible thus far. The deputation was well received, the discussion at the DES was full and copies of the scheme were left for further study - but questions were asked about the cost which seemed to be regarded as somewhat high. The delegation had no problem in justifying its costings and argued that the likely cost of the scheme, when operating in all

380 schools in the county, was equivalent to about 1 per cent (£1.25m) of the LEA's education budget and represented excellent value for money. However, after a wait of several weeks, the answer was negative: funding was available from neither local nor national sources. The teachers' associations had been impressed by the support of both elected members and officers for the view that the level of funding was crucial to the ultimate success of the process.

In line with the policy decision that there would be no further development without adequate financing progress in the field came almost to a halt: officers of the Authority and elected members all honoured their word. However, the working party remained in being to monitor developments elsewhere and to make further preparations in the hope that, at some stage, the climate would change. Indeed, during 1986 things did change, both locally and nationally, not least in relation to the negotiations on teachers' pay and conditions. However, the Cumbria scheme had been agreed locally by all parties and was, as such, regarded by the teachers' associations in the county as binding. Thus, when, in December 1986, the DES invited six local authorities to take part in a pilot project on teacher appraisal, the associations did not hesitate in agreeing that Cumbria should be involved. The working party met and determined that, with funding now available, a smaller group should take on the responsibility for the day to day functioning of the scheme, reporting back only for information or if a policy decision were required. This smaller group, or steering group, was made up of the responsible assistant education officer, the chief inspector/adviser and representatives of the six recognised teachers' associations (NUT, NAS/UWT, AMMA, NATFHE, NAHT and SHA), with an independent chair who had been the headteacher of the comprehensive school which had provided the base career development model from which the Cumbria scheme had evolved. This group was charged with getting the project up and running, including developing a full training package and identifying the schools to take part in the pilot. This was perhaps the most significant development to date as far as the teachers' associations were concerned: it gave them a level of professional involvement that was almost unprecedented, even within Cumbria.

While participation in the national pilot scheme provided access to the long-awaited funding, the view of the teachers' associations was shared by the full working party: 30 schools (six secondary, 24 primary or special) would be sufficient, as opposed to the 45 envisaged in the original phasing plans of the working party. All schools in the county were given the chance to apply for participation in the project, providing that there was full agreement of the teaching staff, following consultation. The steering group received more than three times the number of applications needed and schools were selected to ensure a cross-section of type, size and location and were then placed in three groups, with ten schools in each. Again, control over participation was with the teachers right through to school level.

At the same time, the steering group was developing its requirements for training and it invited both St. Martin's College, Lancaster, and Charlotte Mason College, Ambleside, to tender as providers. There was to be training for heads and co-ordinators for the 'whole school' review element of the project, while both appraisees and appraisers were to have equal access to training, with appraisee training taking place first. All training was preceded by a 'contracting conference' where the details of the scheme and purpose of the national pilot were explained fully. At this stage the project had no co-ordinator and so the steering group took full responsibility for co-ordination while advertising a seconded post as project director head (group 10) for the duration of the pilot - at that stage, until August 1988.

The training programme for both individual teacher appraisal and 'whole school' review was contracted jointly to the two colleges, St. Martin's and Charlotte Mason, working under the direction of the steering group. The main purpose of the training was to equip all those taking part in the pilot with the necessary skills, in particular, the 'appraisal interview' skills for both appraisee and appraiser. The authority policy of a professional development model for teacher appraisal was made very clear to all participants, as was the importance of the pilot being developmental with each cohort of schools informing those that followed.

In order to support the developmental nature of the pilot and to ensure that both the steering group and full working party received appropriate and detailed information, a local evaluation team was formed. It was initially three strong but was, at an early stage, reduced to two: Colin Standing, principal of Kendal College of Further Education, and the author as a representative of the teachers' associations. As evaluators we worked both together and separately, ensuring that all training courses were evaluated and, even more important, that every course member had direct contact with us at the various stages of implementation of the scheme.

The immediate reactions of teachers to the training sessions were extremely positive, although tinged with a cautious view of the future. Full supply cover was provided for the training sessions, which were residential and took place in the comfortable surroundings of a number of Cumbria's hotels. Such accommodation was not only necessary, because of the unavailability of the Authority's own residential training unit, but it also demonstrated the high value put on the whole process of appraisal. At the training sessions it was made clear that this initial quality of provision would be carried through the whole project. Cover was provided to facilitate all stages of the process both for 'whole school' review and individual appraisal, including both provision for teaching analysis and for the appraisal interview.

The whole question of teaching analysis continued to receive considerable attention. The working party accepted that such analysis was central to the appraisal process but also that it must be non-threatening. The observational and analytical process had to be both regular and informal with, in some circumstances, appraiser working alongside appraisee, with both recognising the importance of being constructive and co-operative. Set against such a background, appraisers and appraisees were encouraged to negotiate and agree the criteria on which the analysis was to be structured. While there was some initial apprehension on the part of some appraisees, the outcomes of the initial experiences were positive. As the project was a pilot, it was not possible to develop the 'regular' analysis pattern envisaged by the Cumbria policy, but valuable information was taken forward to inform later cohorts entering the scheme. In particular, there seemed to be considerable value in pitching the 'analysis' process at two levels, the first being general and the second - while still negotiated - being concerned with more specific observations. Other possible difficulties, particularly in the secondary sector, have been identified, arising from the requirement of the Cumbria scheme for the appraiser to be either a head or a deputy, which has clear implications for the time available.

The policy of the Cumbria scheme was that appraisees should have a choice of appraiser, either head or deputy, although in the smallest schools, where there was no deputy, the patch adviser/inspector could be used if a teacher so wished. With the developmental nature of the pilot, it would have been possible to change this approach and there was much discussion about possible alternatives. However, the view of many of the pilot participants was that this represented a particular strength of the scheme - time was set aside when the senior management of the school could be made aware of the detail surrounding the role of individual members of staff. As a result, the steering group has looked at ways of reducing the time load on those senior staff while retaining their direct involvement. Some changes in teaching analysis could provide the answer in this area, although the appraisal cycle in many schools could not be on an annual basis. In fact, the policy envisaged a biennial approach as being appropriate, although within the concept of a continuous cycle. Throughout the pilot no changes were made in policy, although there were developments of the existing policy, all of which had to be agreed at each stage of the administrative structure, thus giving the teachers' associations a high level of control. There was never, as it happened, the need to exercise such a controlling influence, although the active involvement of association representatives ensured that the profession's voice was always heard.

The steering group developed the authority's bid for extension of the pilot work in the academic year 1988-9. The initial bid had been recognised as being closely in line with the Report of the ACAS Appraisal/Training Working Group (1986) and so it was not surprising to find the bid for extension developing some of the particular areas of that Report. Again, the important role played by the teachers' associations in formulating the bid was recognised by all parties and meant that a number of issues relating to the ACAS Report was highlighted. In the light of the expanding scope of the pilot, an assistant project director was appointed.

The question of who appraises whom has already been mentioned and the extension proposed an examination of the extent to which senior teachers and heads of department might be involved in the appraisal process, either as appraisers or in the teaching analysis component. The Authority also proposed to look into how it might be possible to make qualitative judgments of the link between teacher appraisal, 'whole school' review and pupils' learning opportunities. It was recognised that detailed consideration needed to be given to the resource implications and, in particular, to possible refinements to reduce costs - although the steering group insisted that full supply cover must still be provided for training, teaching analysis and the appraisal interview. The extension was also to investigate the links between the identified needs of schools and individuals and INSET provision. Finally, it was proposed to examine the extent to which identified targets were met in respect of professional development. While some new schools were to be introduced, those already involved were to embark upon second appraisal, although the initial rules of voluntary participation remained.

At the same time, the local evaluation team was asked by the steering group to identify positive contributions to learning opportunities that had resulted from the application of the appraisal scheme and, in March 1988, the following 17 items were drawn from evaluation notes.

1. Improvement in the learning environment through more effective use of wall displays.

2. Better integration of current mathematics teaching with that of the previous year group tutor.

3. The ability of teachers to reveal perceived weaknesses in teaching, for which assistance was later forthcoming.

4. Identification of the need for regular, programmed meetings to improve teaching/learning strategies.

5. Improved understanding of the needs of special education and of the teacher concerned.

6. A number of schemes of work was redesigned.

7. In numerous cases curricular deficiencies were identified and remedied, with particular mention made of reading skills, mathematics, science, listening skills and art and craft.

8. Opportunities were taken to observe and adopt the good practice of other teachers.

9. Appraisers and appraisees became better informed about subject areas and initiatives.

10. Some schools improved communication systems, both internal and external.

11. Knowledge of other departments improved the information given to pupils and parents about option choices .

12. The head reverted to the previous class/group organisation, which staff supported - the decision following both 'whole school' review and individual appraisal and being linked to both.

13. Increased involvement of senior management staff in recognising strengths, in using them better and, equally, in recognising problems and helping in their solution. The direct role as appraiser and the function of the 'whole school' review were identified as contributing to this area.

14. Changes were made in classroom organisation as a direct result of an appraisal and, in particular, of the teaching analysis component.

15. Many teachers felt more confident and, as a result, participated more in developing school policy.

16. A number of appraisers identified the revitalising of some colleagues as very significant.

17. Clearer job specification led to more effective understanding of roles and improved organisation in schools.

At this stage it was possible only to identify some immediate effects of the project but, clearly, there were also expectations of some professional development and INSET provision to follow over the coming months. The list was not intended to be exhaustive, but rather to serve as an indicator of positive contributions noted at that stage.

The extension bid was successful and work has since developed in all the areas identified. Significantly, the different form of allocation of INSET money across the county has a direct relationship to the effective provision of INSET needs identified through the appraisal process. In Cumbria, funds in the primary sector are distributed to local consortia, with each deciding the method of further distribution or use. In those consortia where a considerable proportion of the funds is delegated directly for school use it has been possible to target effectively the identified needs arising from either 'whole school' review or individual appraisal. In other consortia there have been more difficulties, particularly where the group's needs did not match individual teacher or school needs. The information will contribute to discussion about the pattern of future arrangements for INSET. At secondary level there have not been similar problems, any difficulties being related to the overall level of funding rather than its management.

An agreed statement results from each individual appraisal. This is part of the process and the statement is available in full only to the appraisee, the appraiser and the head, although agreed information is passed to other appropriate staff, for example, relating to INSET requirements or arrangements for professional development visits to other schools. Ownership of this statement remains with the appraisee: no copy is passed to the Director of Education. The high level of confidentiality has helped build a professional trust that has led to an essentially open and frank exchange of views between appraisees and appraisers.

The original Cumbria scheme emphasised the need for all teachers, including heads, to be included. The initial funding had not allowed the inclusion of heads and the DES was pressed to make an additional allowance to make headteacher appraisal possible. In the view of the steering group, the credibility of the project was at risk if heads of the pilot schools were not appraised. The funding was agreed and a tripartite system was set up to involve the appraisee head, the director's representative (usually the patch adviser) and a colleague head, chosen from a panel, thus replicating as far as possible the element of choice available to other teachers. Although there was some initial apprehension on the part of appraisee heads, the outcomes of the process have been most positive, with all parties expressing support for the approach. The teachers' associations can take some credit for the present success of this part of the scheme because of the reassurance they were able to give colleagues to allay their initial fears.

It must be pointed out that the appraisal scheme is but one of many agreed procedures in Cumbria and must be seen in part in that context. There is an agreed disciplinary procedure, capability procedure, redeployment procedure and staffing re-organised schools procedure, none of which depends upon appraisal. In particular, the Authority recognises that appraisal has no part in determining capability issues. Relationships between the authority and the teachers' associations are good and the director and elected members ensure full consultation, negotiation and involvement in the decision-making process. In particular, teachers have been appreciative of the statements of support from the Authority both during and since the pay and conditions dispute. It is against such a background that teachers have been, and continue to be, supportive of the appraisal scheme.

In considering what features of the Cumbria scheme can be transferred to other Authorities, it is important that any national framework for teacher appraisal should be flexible enough for local negotiation to play its part and that sufficient funds should be available to support locally negotiated schemes. Much, if not all, of what has happened in Cumbria can happen elsewhere and a number of features, all or some of which could be replicated, are as follows:

1. The involvement and commitment of representatives of the elected members wherever possible.

2. The opportunity for teachers, through their professional associations, to model a scheme in co-operation with others.

3. The role of the teachers' associations in evaluating and monitoring the functioning of the scheme.

4. The importance of appropriate training for all teachers, with a recognition that appraisees have the same rights of access to training as appraisers.

5. The authority should give high organisational priority to developing a scheme, with the appointment of appropriate staff to co-ordinate and develop it.

6. The value of having some system of self-review of a 'whole school' as providing the appropriate climate for individual appraisal.

7. The importance of phasing any introduction and regarding it as developmental within the Authority.

8. Arrangements for the meeting of any identified needs, particularly INSET needs.

9. The provision of sufficient time for crucial parts of the scheme to take place within normal school session time - training, teaching analysis/classroom observation, appraisal interview. In such circumstances, some of the less time-demanding components of the process, for example, preparation, discussions/negotiations, feedback on teaching analysis/classroom observation and self-evaluation could be set against other directed time.

10. Provision of supply cover or enhancement of staffing establishments to allow for the session time components listed in 9 above.

11. Any appraisal process must be seen as continuous, with regular discussions and a full appraisal interview/conference at least biennially.

12. Job specification to be provided by heads, after consultation with staff, so that there is an appropriate background to the appraisal.

13. A copy of the agreed procedures should be given to every teacher.

14. Administrative and clerical support is required at Authority and school levels, as any system of appraisal generates additional typing of papers, although not necessarily of any agreed statements.

15. Confidentiality of the statements is crucial and all teachers should know exactly who has access to the agreed statements - in Cumbria, appraisee, appraiser and head have access to the full statement and the LEA requires only limited information, in particular, the date of the last appraisal. Other key staff may need to know specific INSET requirements.

The view in Cumbria throughout the past years has been that appraisal systems must have a positive orientation and that the purpose must be the professional development of teachers. Such development depends upon negotiation and agreement regarding targets, whether for appraisee or appraiser. The fundamental premise has been that individual teacher appraisal and 'whole school' self-evaluation are interlinked and complementary. Teachers' professional development will be most effective if it takes place in tandem with curricular and organisational review, development and self-evaluation of the whole school. Both strands of the scheme inform the INSET needs of the individual, the school, the consortia and the Authority.

Cumbria Local Education Authority has recognised the importance of an effective appraisal process and, by involving fully the representatives of the teachers' associations, has ensured acceptance of the resulting scheme. Over the coming months and years it will be obligatory for all teachers to become involved in a scheme for teacher appraisal and it is my view that only schemes agreed with the profession can succeed in the ultimate aim of enhancing the quality of education. Cumbria LEA and its teachers have developed a model which will continue to be refined but which is to be commended.

Chapter 8

Appraisal in the Inner City

Barbara Payne

It isn't often in the current educational climate that one meets a group of headteachers all of whom are talking about the positive quality of relationships in their schools and discussing the keenness with which their teachers are welcoming a new initiative. I sat in such a meeting recently where ten of the headteachers involved in the appraisal pilot scheme in Newcastle-upon-Tyne were discussing what they required of the LEA as the project comes to an end and they prepare for the second round of appraisals in their schools. There was unanimous conviction that the experience of a quality teacher appraisal process must not be lost in any attempt to slip appraisal in as part of the package of change, without sufficient recognition that only this kind of process will bring long-term and recognisable benefit to schools. Preserving it will require time and resources.

Implicit in that resolve was a sense that there is something to celebrate. I recall that, when a member of staff from my own school returned from a secondment, 'researching' the appraisal scene, he reported that where he had seen appraisal schemes given status and value by the staff, and particularly by the head, you could actually feel something tangibly different when you walked through the front door. A cynic might have been amused at such conversion: now many of us understand exactly what he meant. Now that appraisal has become part of our culture it is possible to reflect a positive effect on the atmosphere and life of the schools involved.

What kind of indicators would we expect to bear such a claim out? If teachers feel valued, do they look happier and more relaxed? If they have been able to disclose something of their own concerns, hopes, aspirations to someone whom they respect and trust, will they be able to empathise more fully with those around them, with friends and strangers alike? If there has been so much emphasis over a protracted period on classroom observation, will the staffroom conversation include more debate about how children learn? Will the relationships formed because of the involvement in the appraisal process last and spread into other areas of the school? Will there be professional concern for all staff where, previously, personality got in the way? Will it be possible for a stranger to walk into the school and sense that something excitingly different is going on and comment on it? Will there be 'spin offs' into other areas of education that could not have been foreseen in the beginning? The list of possibilities is endless. I would give a resounding affirmative to all these questions. It has happened. There is evidence to substantiate the claims.

In case any 'alienation effect' is taking place, at this point I should explain that I am not claiming a miracle or transformation, but simply that there is significant development of a kind that is worth investigation.

Before us runs the swift, relentless millstream of educational reform and I am looking at teacher appraisal with an inner city perspective which brings its own currents, turbulence and demand.

A city like Newcastle-upon-Tyne is a place of marked contrasts and considerable apparent affluence. On any Saturday morning, accompany me to the food hall of Marks & Spencer. There you will get some idea of the extent to which low housing costs, in comparison with the rest of the country, provide more than 60 per cent of the population with a considerable amount of disposable income. Listen to local industrialists, witness the Japanese investment in the north-east and you might be tempted to think that paradise is regained.

The fascination for those of us who live our lives in cities is to do with diversity and mix. Newcastle provides cultural riches - opera and the Royal Shakespeare Company - and access to the wonderful countryside of Northumberland, North Yorkshire and the Lakes; but these opportunities live side by side with poverty, limited horizons and blatant despair. There are parts of Newcastle which reveal the dark side of the moon. Houses are boarded up, businesses closed down, litter and graffiti illustrate the familiar symptoms of inner city decay and social decline.

City Profiles - the results of the 1986 Housing Survey - provided stark facts and the situation has got worse since they were produced. When they were published, male unemployment was running at 27 per cent, youth unemployment was running at 50 per cent - situations familiar in many large, northern cities and towns. Untypically, Newcastle has a community where 97 per cent of households has as head of household 'a person of European origin', three per cent of the total population of the city is represented by a small Asian and a smaller Chinese community. Teaching against this background of decided tension and contrast is as complex and demanding as it is in other major conurbations.

As a manager of a large school (perhaps it is of even more concern in a small school), one cannot fail to register the accumulating effect of the explosion of new legislation which is calling for significant change in many aspects of school life. It is worth recognising the psychology of organisations and understanding that, for a very small minority of people within any organisation, change is welcome and regarded as exciting. More significantly, it is important to register the fact that for the majority of people change is unpleasant, threatening and stressful.

Anyone with eyes to see can also observe the accumulating outcome of that stress in schools. Of course, stress is necessary and enjoyable in some aspects of its manifestations but when it spills over it causes problems for the organisation as well as for the individual. For decades it has been unacceptable for teachers to admit to weakness. There are a variety of reasons for this, including the simple concept that big boys (and girls) don't cry. Teachers struggle on in comparative isolation. If one looks at the absence returns for staff over the past few years in any school, it is more than likely that there will be an increased level of absence caused by the number of staff experiencing long-term depressive illnesses, staff with serious back injuries and damaged joints and a preponderance of medical certificates which refer to mysterious viral or post-viral symptoms. I have undertaken such an analysis in my own school and find convincing evidence that stress is the cause. Staff absence can be cumulative when it puts more strain on those in reasonable health and creates a 'domino' effect. This presents a significant organisational problem, threatens curriculum continuity and makes it more urgent that we find a systematic remedy.

The reasons for this depressing profile are self-evident to those of us working in, or closely with, schools but sadly not to the letter writers in our local paper, one of whom suggested recently that teachers should be organised into night shifts to patrol the school buildings and grounds in order to keep vandalism down!

An additional pressure every teacher will recognise is the expectation by society at large that schools should somehow solve the problems created by economic and social circumstances beyond their control. In addition, the constant level of criticism directed at the profession from people who should know better is, in its milder forms, wearing and, in its bolder presentations, deeply offensive. It is in no way helpful to see the Secretary of State's correspondence with local LEAs reported in the newspapers. His concern for the success of a Buckingham Palace garden party to celebrate 150 years of state education was expressed through a warning that LEAs should send only people who would know how to behave themselves. The implication is obvious, the retraction apology which followed irrelevant. If the teaching profession is not valued by those in charge, what is there to celebrate? There is a whole range of reasons why the raising of the profession must come from within. Time is, I know, at a premium in schools. There is never enough of it. The teacher's role has extended to encompass so many responsibilities that teachers feel they are failing even when they are making heroic efforts and working impossible hours, and even when they are providing the kind of positive learning experiences which children will recall in later life. Teachers need recognition from their profession and from their schools for what they are achieving now. In partnership they need to celebrate it, if there is to be any hope of improved quality of experience in the classroom.

If you accept this scenario even partially, then it is possible that you will also agree that it is of vital importance that we bring about a 'sea change', that we provide in schools the kind of environment where it is acceptable for teachers to admit to vulnerability and even despair, occasionally to take risks and maybe get things wrong, but through which they will be supported intellectually and emotionally. If there can be no recognition from without at present, then there can be a sense of developing value from within. It may be that the teaching profession then becomes a force to be reckoned with and society will view us accordingly.

All these considerations were in the forefront of our minds when, at Kenton, the school where I am head, we decided to investigate, for human and organisational reasons, the need for a structured developmental system for staff, later to be called the appraisal system. It is interesting to record that, although there is now a widespread involvement of schools in this Authority at primary, special and middle school levels, the early work began at Kenton. Soon after our work began in earnest, in the autumn of 1986, the opportunity arose for the LEA to become involved in the national pilot scheme and it was decided to base the project at Kenton, with the senior teacher who had developed our planning within the school becoming the project coordinator.

Kenton is a large school on a sprawling campus, catering for 1,600 pupils with 100 teaching staff and three staffrooms. The school was developed on one site but from three separate school buildings. It is well subscribed. Last year's intake of approximately 300 pupils ranged from six pupils with a reading age of six, to ten pupils who on cognitive testing were identified as 'more able'. A visiting HMI commented that it was a long time since he had been in a school catering for such a wide range of abilities. In many ways the school reflects the contrasts and paradoxes of the city itself. This is borne out in the way that the Kenton profile of statistics reflects the norm position which conceals a wide range of conditions. The same HMI, after two days in the area, presumably acknowledging 'the urban edge', asked if we ever felt we were holding back the thin red line. Those of us too young to be readily familiar with wartime metaphors were still able to ponder what the nature of the imagined invasion might be. Our conclusion was that there is no evidence in the school, and certainly none detected by parents who choose the school, that we are regarded as having any 'front line' characteristics - but it was an interesting question.

There have always been comments from visitors about the school's friendliness, the relaxed atmosphere, the sense of accessibility and the commitment to teaching and learning. Much of this has been actively encouraged in an attempt to create an appropriately welcoming atmosphere and a comfortable and stimulating environment in which pupils and staff can work. Above all, it is an open and responsive community. It would be foolish, however, to ignore what is going on in the diverse communities outside the school. It would also be wrong to assume that we are a cosy haven. Our work is rooted in the reality with which and within which we work.

As a head, I would put relationship and team building high on my management agenda and therefore put great store by the comment made by Keith Ridyard, the appraisal co-ordinator, in his article, 'The human touch' (1989), in which he says:

> 'Our experience to date, in preparing teachers for appraisal, would suggest that it is possible to de-mystify the concept of relationship building in order that the elements which are crucial to constructive dialogue can be digested by both appraiser and appraisee.'

It is a claim which needs investigating but it is fundamental to the nature of the work in which we are engaged.

First, a brief look back to how it all began, which is difficult because many of us have become so immersed in the process and (regrettably) the jargon of appraisal that it is hard to 'disaggregate' (a word I have borrowed from LMS terminology). In retrospect, one can see that the appropriate 'climate setting' was created by the introduction of opportunities for both institutional and individual development arising out of a kind of natural progression.

By the summer of 1986 the school, collectively and through wide-ranging discussions, had undergone a review of its aims and objectives and a review of its curriculum. The curriculum group, comprised mainly of heads of department, had devised an evaluation and assessment policy for the school, producing guidelines on marking, schemes of work, examinations and reporting procedures. This had been an exciting experience as the group struggled towards forming 'whole school' policies which were then given to the staff for open debate and approval. All this was good preparation for what was to come. The next logical step was into staff development. First, we looked at what should be taught, then at how it was being taught. Inevitably, while we were considering these issues, the focus moved to the teachers themselves, their need for support and encouragement and a sense of purpose. As an experiment, a course was devised, entitled 'Preparation for promotion'. This offered the staff for the first time an opportunity to look at the roles and responsibilities of members of the management team, heads of department, year tutors and others and to consider how to prepare for their own next career move in general terms, in terms of course preparation and reading and in the more specific areas of preparing for an interview, filling in application forms and general preparedness. The hidden agenda of the course itself was the opening up of the organisation for exploration and review. This was a voluntary course held after school for six sessions and about 40 of the staff participated.

As a result of the course, provision was made for an intrepid, self-selecting group of staff to experience a simulated interview and to be provided by the head with detailed feedback on their individual performance and how they had been assessed by the interviewing committee. This committee had been chosen from a group of people not closely connected with the school and with whom staff would not necessarily come in contact in the search for promotion. It proved a fascinating experience for all participants. It was interesting to observe how staff prepared themselves and how real the pre-interview nerves were. Many of those involved said afterwards that this was the best bit of staff development in which they had been involved, primarily because they felt they had been stretched and made to think about themselves but they had felt supported through the process. There were important messages here. This positive experience combined with the feeling within the school that much had been done to establish a climate in which staff development could blossom and be appreciated and teachers now understood their need for personal and professional development.

Ironically, at this stage the teachers' unions were promoting in a variety of publications the idea of establishing appraisal systems in schools for the reasons just referred to. There was a climate of greater accountability and papers such as *Teaching Quality* (DES 1983) and *Better Schools* (DES 1985) were calling for better knowledge of teacher performance. All these factors pointed the way.

There were several phases to our introduction of appraisal. The first could be called the 'information gathering stage'. It was decided that a member of the school management team should be seconded for the summer term 1986 to investigate what was going on in the general area of staff development and appraisal, both in education and industry. Although much was being written and developed throughout the country, at this time our knowledge extended to the work of the Industrial Society, that of David Trethowan (1987) and more locally of Richard Houlden.

When the secondment ended we were provided with much more accurate information. Of particular interest was the target-setting system operated at Proctor and Gamble, which influenced early thinking. As a result of sharing this information, there was general consensus among the staff that we should design a system of appraisal for Kenton which was both suitable and acceptable. A strong emphasis was given then, and has been maintained since, that teachers need to feel 'ownership' of the system. Obviously, the teachers at Kenton, like teachers in any school, reflected a spectrum of attitude and opinion in the light of this proposal. There were those who were distinctly suspicious, sceptical, uninterested, some tacitly and some outspokenly but the majority were voluble in their support and enthusiasm.

The management structure at Kenton may appear less hierarchical than in some schools. It has been my aim since taking up the headship to tap the innovation, energy and vigour of young teachers and not to rely solely on the perspective of the few. The management team itself had been widened to include senior teachers and their job specification has tended to shift from operation 'control' mechanisms to responsibilities rooted within the curriculum.

It was therefore against the background of seeking to encourage teachers to participate in developing policy that it was agreed to set up the appraisal working group to devise a scheme and report back to staff. This represents the second stage of appraisal implementation - the 'planning stage'.

The kind of group that was set up represented a complete departure from previous development groups and was to prove the model on which the future management of the school was to depend. Somewhat influenced by the concept of quality circles, the group represented a vertical slice of the school hierarchy from probationer teacher to head (who was not in the chair). There was representation from each of the three staffrooms, from the teaching unions and a reasonable balance of the sexes and areas of the curriculum. The teachers involved were specifically invited to join the group because of the particular strengths most of them held as communicators on the informal networks of the school, being people, in the main, with 'staffroom credibility'. After initial awareness-training, the group developed a powerful dynamic and quickly both the process and the underpinning philosophy emerged.

The third stage was the development of a clear philosophy which could be used as a sounding board and which could be checked out with staff before proceeding further. Appraisal was to be teacher-owned. The process was all important. All aspects of that process were to be negotiated. The focus was to be the professional discussion between appraisee and appraiser. The appraiser was to be someone who would take on responsibility for the vital follow-up and review. Careful preparation for self-appraisal was necessary if real benefit from the discussion was to ensue. Everyone involved in the process needed training. The important emphasis was on relationship-building. Trust and confidence needed to be established before staff would view classroom observation with equanimity. It was also established that, whereas this might be the blueprint for Kenton, other schools would need to work through the issues and develop their own 'bespoke' system if they were to feel genuine ownership.

The basis on which these issues were revised was Keith Ridyard's secondment report - familiarly known as the Grey Book, its formal title being *Teacher Appraisal - An Approach*. The strength of this document was that it raised and confronted all the issues connected with teachers' hopes, fears and aspirations. It did not set them aside or dismiss them. It raised key issues and allowed teachers to work them through. Many of the questions raised are still the key issues for us all - especially those which asked about the direct correlation between the amount of time to be given to the process and the quality of the experience.

Once the philosophy emerged, there was a significant fourth stage in our implementation plan and that was quite simply consultation and a recognition that time was needed to reflect on and test out what was beginning to be formulated. This was critical to the process of the development of a scheme and also this was the crucial stage in convincing staff that they had ownership, that this was to be their scheme.

Whereas others may have decided to adopt a more unequivocal stance, we were clear that the Grey Book was a working document and that there was likely to be a great deal of thinking revision and reworking of the initial documentation. That was part of the message gleaned from industries: many companies taking appraisal seriously were into their ninth draft. In fact, the Grey Book was completely replaced in 1987 by the STAFF (School Teacher Appraisal Formative Framework) Manual and Action Plan. These documents have also been under constant review and revision as the project has widened, more schools have come into the project and modifications have been found necessary in the light of practical experience. There have been six major revisions of the documentation which is once again under complete revision, consideration being given now to a new format to communicate the message of the project as the pilot study comes to an end. This is one example of the extent to which our experience has emphasised the process and the need for constant reflection and refinement. The opportunity for this came about when the teachers' unions decided to adopt an uncooperative stance towards appraisal in the pilot Authorities. Those of us who respected, but did not agree with, their reasons for doing so did not seek to create tension between teachers' loyalty to their unions and to their schools, nor to cause any crisis of conscience.

Teachers found acceptable the concept that they could acquire the skills without engaging in actual appraisal and as such stay within union guidelines. As ours was a 'whole school' approach, we maintained that position as long as was possible, a decision which delayed the process but did not damage it. For the majority of staff at Kenton, appraisal was never seen as a union issue, since a commitment had been given before the dispute. However, union circumstances in Newcastle did, for some time, prevent primary school involvement in the scheme. Many primary teachers were impatient with the stance adopted and wanted to test the system. It was a difficult judgment to make, but the decision to tread delicately resulted in a considerable delay between training and 'live' appraisal, a situation fortunately not experienced by schools coming into the project at a later stage.

Now that there was a coherent and identifiable philosophy, we moved into the fifth stage of development - the area of training. During this period it was possible to concentrate on 'in-depth' training in all aspects of the process. Particularly memorable and effective was the training in feedback and reviewing skills which were to prove such a vital part of successful appraisal and which have been transferred into other aspects of school life with noticeable effect.

Training was carried out initially by members of CCDU (Careers and Counselling Development Unit) based at Leeds, whose style and philosophy seemed very much in tune with our own. Gradually, as the project developed, and while still valuing the consultancy of a few of the original trainers, the LEA developed its own team of trainers, initially trained by CCDU, who worked first as co-trainers and then in their own right and who now form a powerful resource for the LEA. It is interesting to note that some of these trainers are teachers from Kenton who were either members of the appraisal working group or who participated in the early appraisal rounds.

During this fallow period there was continuous discussion and debate about the nature of the system. Careful consideration was given to loading words with messages that were in tune with the philosophy: thus, it was not to be an 'appraisal interview' but a 'professional discussion', not 'classroom observation' but 'action research into learning'. There was general concern to remove any judgmental overtones. Of course, during this time other schools were also undergoing awareness-raising and training and the role of the co-ordinator and assistant co-ordinator in maintaining impetus at this stage of the project was never more apparent.

When the training was undertaken at Kenton, 40 teachers (not the same 40 as on the preparation for promotion course) volunteered to be part of initial appraiser training. Because of the definition of 'appraiser' training, this group represented most of those in senior and middle management of the school. There was a two day awareness-raising residential course at the Durham Business School, followed by a one-day follow-up course. In between, some training staff were required, after some preliminary training in technique, to try out classroom observation by negotiating in pairs a focus for observation and to extend their understanding of observational techniques by 'doing'. Training for this emphasised the importance of a trusting, empathetic relationship between observer and observed. Techniques of observation were exemplified, including the use of the observation as part of self-evaluation.

If I were to pinpoint any time during the pilot scheme when the school was animated and alive in a new dimension, it was during that particular fortnight between elements of training. It was not so much a 'coming out' as a 'going in'. For the first time the isolation of the secondary teacher in the classroom was broken down. This was not an inspectoral visit from adviser, HMI or college lecturer but a colleague negotiating why, carrying out an observation from which both parties were to learn more about their craft, opening up the fascinating issues surrounding how and why students learn and raising questions as to why they do not. It was now that the conversation in the staffrooms changed radically. It couldn't have been otherwise. Teachers were daily making new discoveries about the work in which they were involved. The staffroom, the corridors and the classrooms were humming with a sense of a different kind of industry and focus. Looking back and reflecting on what went on, it is quite clear that we learnt a variety of lessons from the implementation process itself.

There was, I suggest, a sense in which those not involved, even the most disaffected, became envious. This is an interesting factor to bear in mind when bringing about change. It was therefore doubly unfortunate that there was a considerable delay, for reasons already indicated, before it was possible to proceed with actual appraisal discussions. Inevitably, the effect of some of the early training wore off. People recede to their natural, instinctive style. This was clearly far from ideal and, in the later stages of the project's development, great care has been given to see that experience of 'real' appraisal (I baulk at the term 'live' which had some currency in the early stages) should directly follow the training experience.

A further illumination has been the sense in which we now understand better how Kenton 'works'. Part of the enlightenment within the school which has taken place has been to understand more fully the complicated psychology of the organisation and more consideration has been given to why people behave in particular ways. The appraisal group was keen to examine precisely and sensitively how staff were feeling and reacting at each stage, both as individuals and as groups. It was therefore possible to develop strategies which both 'coaxed and coached' people along the way. Managing any kind of change is a complex task and lessons learned through this experience have been extremely useful in wider contexts and as the rate of change has accelerated in complementary areas of school life.

When real appraisal started, more than a year later than originally intended, in May 1988, ten appraisees went through the process. It was the headteacher's responsibility to organise the pairing and check out its acceptability with both partners. On the whole a line management structure was emerging but, because of the development of cross-curricular responsibilities within the school organisation, it was by no means universal that each teacher was appraised by someone from his/her own subject area. Therefore, another lesson we learned was that it was not appropriate to make assumptions about line management in secondary schools. The final picture is more complex and in a sense we have learned that this issue is not so crucial to the process as the quality of the appraisal itself.

The process of appraisal we adopted is not markedly different from that operating elsewhere. The elements we felt to be absolutely essential were the opportunity for self-appraisal and preparation before the professional discussion itself, the provision of effective follow up and review and, above all, the significance of setting mutually negotiated targets.

The process was tightly structured. An initial meeting between the two teachers was called to set the agenda, organise the venue and ensure the information collection. The collecting of information was agreed and it was to be carried out jointly in an attempt to provide a two-way perspective. It was hoped that this would enable the appraisee to go more confidently into the professional discussion and would assist the appraiser in providing accurate feedback. Whatever information was gathered was to be relevant to the past year. Individual teachers were to be encouraged to keep a record of anything relevant during the year ahead to facilitate the next appraisal cycle and to ensure that recognition of success and identification of development needs were not overlooked. It was part of the agreed process that appraisers should take the opportunity to discuss informally with colleagues relevant information concerning an area of additional responsibility which could be as a form teacher, as a manager, or in teaching a second subject. The purpose of this was to assist in the whole process of self-appraisal and allow a wider scope for the professional discussion. In addition, it was important to record feedback from action research into learning. All this information would be included on the pre-professional preparation form which the appraisee would hand to the appraiser before the discussion.

Staff had also been given a variety of trigger mechanisms, from drawing their own 'road maps' to filling in self awareness forms, both within earlier training and now at the focal point of the appraisal process to aid them in self reflection. It was curious how difficult most secondary teachers found it to express themselves visually rather than in words, as required on some of the training exercises. This activity many teachers found difficult and new, but infinitely rewarding.

All this, in preparation for the professional discussion training, had underlined the importance of timing and ambience. Consideration was to be given as to when and where the appraisee would feel most comfortable. Obviously, as part of a pilot project, supply cover was available. There were resources to support the process 'in all its aspects'. This meant not only that status was given to the process but also that discussions were able to run their full course. They usually fell within a range of two to five hours. Considerable emphasis was placed on the joint nature of the responsibility. There was to be no fixed agenda but there was a simple structure on which to hang the discussion: What has gone well for you? What has not gone so well? Where do we go from here? What targets shall we agree for the future? After the discussion the appraiser was to draft a summary of it which, when agreed, would be written up on the forms provided. Each would keep a copy and a copy would go to the headteacher. These documents were to be confidential and not available in any other context. One thing which we did not realise at the outset was that writing up the documentation required particular skills. Many staff found it difficult to précis the discussion; some sought to capture its essence by recalling verbatim what was said. The problem facing all staff was precisely what to record. 'We both had a favourable reaction to the lesson observed and felt it went as planned' was too generalised and did not infer that much meaningful discussion had taken place about the precise nature of the learning experience. 'He asked that we should examine all aspects of his role within the school and tease out both his strengths and weaknesses, which we proceeded to do painstakingly', gives more of an idea of what actually happened but does not suggest how valuable the two people involved found the experience nor the quality of the disclosure.

Similar difficulty was found when setting targets. Some, taken out of context, appear almost humorous - 'to maintain and possibly improve the female response to my subject' - because of their vague nature. Some staff took readily to the need to be realistic and precise, as indicated in the following set of targets:

- To establish an action plan for implementing a new project.
- To arrange a meeting for interested teachers in the next few weeks.
- To follow this meeting with 3 x 1 hour training sessions.
- To try out ideas with pupils in the spring term.

How to write the records is still an area that needs clarification and work is going on to provide guidelines, if not a formula, to reduce the length of the documentation which has emerged and to provide actual 'training' in the essentials of appraisal record-keeping.

There was a great deal of apprehension and expectation as the first ten appraisals took place. Everyone wanted to give of his/her best. There was also, in spite of all effort to the contrary, a great deal of pressure. Self appraisal cast everyone into the philosophic mode but feelings before the professional discussion were tense and both appraisees and appraisers admitted to nerves.

When the process was over the ten appraisees were called together to see how they felt the experience had gone. Where target setting was relevant, precise and real, appraisees appeared to be energised by the experience. The appraisers were called together later that same week and were given feedback from the appraisee meeting by members of the appraisal working group who had been present at both meetings. It was explained to them that there was no sense in which anyone was being required to disclose what was said but merely how they felt. The appraisees were exceedingly open and frank.

Out of the ten, seven were very appreciative of the experience: 'It was the first time I really felt valued in my entire career'; 'To spend two hours talking about *me* was wonderful'. These were some of the most enthusiastic and endearing responses. Of the three who were slightly more cautious, one commented that the process was a bit too comfortable and informal and another felt that she had not really gained much from the process. After some reflection and after listening to what the appraisers had to say, it became clear that where there was dissatisfaction it was caused by three particular factors. First, the appraiser had not used the guidelines and had not structured the discussion sufficiently to allow discussion to flow. Experience has shown that the appraiser needs to do a considerable amount of preparation in ensuring the structure of the discussion, while allowing it to be flexible and to include input from the appraisee. Practice led to improvement but the other two problems were more difficult to address, particularly the emphasis on making the process bias free.

One of the results of our insisting that the whole process should not be judgmental meant that some appraisees felt that they were not given sufficient insights into their classroom management. They actually wanted views, values and opinions. It was necessary to reconsider the extent to which it was possible or desirable never to bring values and judgment into the process and a decision was taken that what mattered was how judgment was introduced and issues were raised. It was recognised that, if development was to take place, then teachers needed help with analysing where their technique was failing; a pivotal balance between support and criticism needed to be established and could only work when the relationship allowed.

The last factor which emerged was much more difficult to handle and one which any organisation may have difficulty in resolving, namely, where there is an intellectual mismatch between appraisee and appraiser which leads to disappointment, especially for the appraisee, if the discussion does not take place at a sufficiently sophisticated level of debate.

It was of great importance that we gained such full disclosure about the process at this time for it enabled the project immediately to confront the issues arising from it and to learn from mistakes made in these first trials. It was also interesting to observe that, where an appraisee felt things had not gone as well as hoped and high expectations had been generated, so too the appraiser felt disappointed and absorbed the burden of responsibility for not providing the best for his/her appraisee. It was in ways like this that the 'demystifying of relationships', referred to earlier, began. Somehow, the appraisal structure depersonalised things in the sense that original reactions/reservations to possible pairings, born out of historic attitudes, personality conflicts and other matters, receded. Obviously, the pairing had been carried out with some sensitivity to these issues. Original concerns about 'who my appraiser would be' disappeared. In fact, it is true to say that this has not been raised as an issue since that time and seems to have been replaced by a genuine concern to provide the best for whoever one is paired with within the process. I like to believe that professionalism and integrity came to the fore. What was also important was that the whole organisation was learning from the experience.

By the time the second cycle of appraisals started the participants had absorbed the lessons of the first round. On reflection, we identified that the concept of 'coaching' was vital here. Some of the initial appraisers who had lacked confidence, aided by the diplomatic intervention of the co-ordinator, by discussion and through protracted counselling, were now able to provide an improved experience for the second phase of appraisees.

A joint meeting of appraisers and appraisees was held after the second cycle of appraisals. Teachers were again more than willing to give feedback to each other. One of the phrases used by a trainee in the early stages, 'Give me feedback without destroying me', has passed into jocular, staffroom currency but indicates a new sensitivity in our treatment of each other in the pressured environment of school where it is so easy to personalise, take offence or feel threatened when we are tired or overworked. Thus appraisal has been a civilising process.

As each of the five cycles of appraisals was completed there were fewer criticisms of the process and what disappointments and difficulties have occurred have been taken up on a personal, individual level, so no one has remained unsupported, however insignificant the level of disappointment. The majority view is still that appraisal has offered the best opportunity yet to feel valued, recognised and supported.

Appraisers have felt more confident, if more aware of the time-consuming nature of their responsibilities. In the emphasis on the importance of follow-up and review, the full brunt of responsibility has been realised. It is difficult to sustain qualitative involvement through five appraisals. It has certainly convinced those of us managing the system that the number of appraisals carried out by any one appraiser must be limited if we are to maintain the level of disclosure and the quality of relationships which exist now. During the fourth and fifth cycles of appraisal taking place at Kenton in late 1988/early 1989 it became timely to carry out interim follow-up review for those who had been appraised in the early appraisal cycles. This does need to be given consideration by those planning a school appraisal system and points to the necessity for co-ordination and monitoring to take place at senior levels within LEA management structures.

As we look back to our involvement in setting up the appraisal system and start planning what is possible in the post pilot year ahead, one thing is certain: appraisal has released a diverse range of emotions. It has been an exhausting experience precisely because of the levels of emotional energy invested. It is right to register the level of fatigue which may also be predictable at this stage of implementation and after all the excitement of the early innovations.

As the lead school in the pilot scheme, we have, of course, been subject to considerable scrutiny both from within the LEA, by our own evaluator and from those co-ordinating and evaluating the project nationally, from HMI and from LEAs interested in finding out what has been going on. We have also been involved in videos made by the LEAP project and in producing our own video jointly with Focus in Education. All this could have led to the kind of over-exposure which causes not only fatigue but a loss of freshness and a loss of commitment to the central purpose. Thankfully, none of this appears to have happened.

One of the problems we are left with as an organisation is how to get the momentum operating on a 'manageable' level. It is clear that we cannot sustain much further the intense level of activity and input that characterised the development phase of the appraisal system. There is bound to be a 'levelling out' but we hope that it will be possible to retain the quality of the experience in the process.

What certainly remains is the constant commitment and enthusiasm from the staff who have participated, which has been reinforced through experience, and an understanding by a wide range of teachers that any organisation which does not have good relationships will find difficulty confronting all that is required of it in the future. What also remains is the expectation of teachers who are yet to participate that things will be good for them too.

The prevailing good humour of those involved is another characteristic I will cherish in the future. It has underpinned the development work. We have learned to laugh at ourselves, to relax and to note the absurdities of everyday life and of the 'mission impossible', which is our brief as teachers, without ever deflecting our serious commitment which is to improve the quality of learning for the pupils in our care.

Hopefully, too, what is left is a strong sense of fellowship within the school, recognisable by those from the outside, which gives us all a sense of purpose and a sense of achievement and proves that appraisal has brought about in Kenton School a significant cultural change. If teachers are beginning to feel valued here and are strengthened by the experience, and if other schools all over the country recognise the central significance of this type of appraisal system, then there just might be something genuine and tangible to celebrate in the next 150 years of publicly provided education.

Chapter 9

Evaluation and the Teaching Profession

Linda Darling-Hammond

Personnel evaluation reveals what is valued in an organisation, how roles are construed and which goals have *de facto* priority in the management of organisational affairs. The importance attached to this function says much about the organisation's relationships among its members. The same can be said about the importance of evaluation in an occupation whose members share a common service mission. Indeed, evaluation plays a particularly critical role in an occupation that claims to be a profession. This chapter explores the role of teacher evaluation in school organisations and in the teaching occupation. It argues for a more professional approach to the evaluation of teaching and discusses how professionalism through evaluation may be achieved.

Teacher evaluation can be utterly unimportant. In many school districts it is a perfunctory bureaucratic requirement that yields little help for teachers and little information on which a school district can base decisions. Teachers anticipate a brief annual visit from the principal, who, according to the stereotype, stands stonefaced at the back of the classroom filling in a form. And principals rush to squeeze in their visits to teachers amid their myriad other duties. Hurried conferences are held and forms are filled and signed. The exercise does little for teachers except contribute to their weariness and reinforce their scepticism of bureaucratic routine. Isolated from decision-making and planning, the exercise does little for administrators except add to their workload. It does not provide a mechanism for a school system to communicate its expectations concerning teaching, except that teaching is a fair subject for bureaucratisation.

In recent years, a number of changes in traditional teacher evaluation practices has been proposed as policy makers have sought to find ways to screen out less competent teachers and to reward the more competent. These changes have tended to create more elaborate evaluation procedures - adding more required observations, more evaluators and more conferences and documentation. The search for more objective evaluation instruments has also pushed ahead, with efforts to articulate in checklist form those aspects of teacher behaviour found in some research to be related to teacher effectiveness. In the most fundamental sense, though, these efforts, by and large prove the old saying: 'Plus ça change, plus c'est la méme chose.' The common and unchanged features of teacher evaluation systems are those that are central to a bureaucratic conception of teaching work: (1) evaluation is designed and conducted chiefly by administrators ; (2) ratings are based on a few inspections of classroom activities; (3) standardised checklists based on standardised criteria are used to record generic kinds of teacher behaviour and to derive ratings (which, on a three- or five-point scale, are intended to reflect relative performance); (4) all teachers are evaluated on a common schedule (generally once a year) using the common instrument and uniform procedures; (5) this standardised process is intended to serve simultaneously as the primary vehicle for discussions of individual teaching practice, for professional development guidance and for personnel decision-making.

The bureaucratic concept of teaching implies that administrators and specialists plan the curriculum, and teachers implement a curriculum planned for them. Teachers' work is supervised by superiors whose job it is to make sure that teachers implement the curriculum and procedures of the school district. In the pure bureaucratic concept, teachers do not plan or inspect their work; they merely perform it.

In a more professional concept of teaching, teachers plan, conduct and evaluate their work both individually and collectively. They analyse the needs of their students, assess the resources available, take the school district's goals into account and decide on their instructional strategies. They conduct instruction, modifying their strategies to make sure that their instruction meets the needs of their students. And through a variety of means they assess whether or not students have learned. Evaluation of teaching is conducted largely to ensure that proper standards of practice are being employed.

These differing concepts of teaching lead to very different approaches to teacher evaluation. Paradoxically, while discussions of and experiments with new forms of evaluation are occurring (e.g. efforts to involve peers in the process), the bureaucratic features of teacher evaluation are becoming more widespread and less open to challenge, as many state legislatures mandate teacher evaluation practices based on this model.

It is the bureaucratic concept of teacher evaluation - and these resulting features of evaluation processes - that limit its validity for assessing teacher performance and its usefulness for improving teaching. As a consequence, the traditional approach to teacher evaluation offers little hope for developing professional accountability in teaching.

Furthermore, professional accountability mechanisms and evaluation practices in other professions include none of the common features of traditional teacher evaluation. Indeed, although evaluation occurs in a variety of forms, there is no direct counterpart in other professions to what we think of as teacher evaluation. After presenting the modes and rationales for the very different evaluation approaches in other professions, I shall explore an alternative approach to evaluation as it might operate in a teaching profession rather than in an instructional bureaucracy.

The primary criticism of traditional teacher evaluation practices is that they are, by their very design, largely incapable of providing worthwhile insights into teacher competence and the appropriateness of teaching practice beyond the identification of those teachers who lack the most rudimentary teaching skills. Constructive evaluation would provide an assessment of teaching that reveals not only whether or not a teacher does specific things at certain times (e.g. whether or not a teacher has lesson plans, behavioural objectives, and an orderly classroom during the two periods a year when the evaluator appears) but whether a teacher has sufficient knowledge, skill, and judgment to make sound teaching decisions over a sustained period on behalf of many students with diverse needs. The former is required of a teaching bureaucrat. The latter is what is required of a teaching professional.

This is not to say that important insights into the qualities of teachers and teaching do not sometimes occur in schools. However, they generally do not occur within the context of, or as a result of, the teacher evaluation system. Feedback from parents and students and impressions gained from the limited interactions among school staff contribute to perceptions of teachers and teaching quality. However, these 'external' observations are not useful for personnel decision-making when acceptable data can be derived only from the prescribed evaluation procedures. The validity of such observations is questionable because they arise haphazardly, often by hearsay, and with no obvious route into the decision-making process. Moreover, whatever administrators learn about teachers' performances has little influence on general teaching practice because the evaluation process is limited to a few interactions between individual teachers and their evaluator(s) and focuses on discrete incidents of teaching behaviour.

How does it happen that many of the most important aspects of teaching - and the most important goals of evaluation - prove unreachable through traditional teacher evaluation processes? First, bureaucracies, especially public bureaucracies, are compelled at least to appear to be treating all employees alike. If some teachers are to be evaluated each year, then all teachers must be evaluated in exactly the same manner each year. This leaves less time for principals to meet the formal requirement, and the result is usually not a thorough and relevant assessment of all teachers but a perfunctory one. Because many do not believe that the formal requirement will lead to decisions anyway, school systems do not invest sufficiently in the process. Hence, the circular and ironic result is *pro forma* evaluation - producing results that are not sufficiently reliable and valid to be used for personnel decisions. Because there are usually neither additional evaluation time nor resources available to support teachers having difficulty, the opportunity for improvement and the requirement to follow the procedures are not met.

The problems inherent in assigning the teacher evaluation function solely to principals are evident. Principals have little time for evaluation and they have a wide span of control. A typical principal has from 20 to 100 teachers to supervise, as compared to the supervisory ration of no more than 1 to 10 in most other types of organisations. Principals also report that they often experience 'role conflict' as they try to balance their roles as school leaders, supervisors and builders of *esprit de corps*. But most important, principals cannot have specialised subject matter or pedagogical knowledge of all teaching areas in which they are expected to evaluate teachers . The limits on their time and expertise and on the tools available to them mean that principals can, at best, assess whether the teachers in their charge are minimally competent.

Evaluation of minimal competence , based on periodic observations of classroom performance, attends to the presence of certain generic teaching behaviours that nearly all teachers except the incompetent will exhibit (e.g., Does the teacher plan? Set objectives? Teach to the objectives? Establish and enforce rules for student behaviour?). This type of evaluation does not attend to matters of pedagogical knowledge or judgment, such as the appropriateness of teaching objectives for meeting certain goals or for different types of students; the appropriateness of the goals themselves; the relative effectiveness of alternative strategies for presenting particular types of content; the relationship among lessons taught throughout the course of a week, a month, or a term; the variability of teaching techniques; the theoretical soundness of content and strategy decisions; or the depth of subject matter knowledge the teacher possesses and imparts to students.

Because the evaluator is not usually an expert in the teaching area, and the criteria are generalised so as to apply, at least superficially, to all teaching areas, there is little capacity in the typical evaluation system for assessing the appropriateness of observed teaching behaviours. Evaluation can attend only to the form rather than the substance of teaching and to the immediate rather than the long-term effects of teaching.

These limitations are compounded by the reliance on classroom observations (and only a few of these at most) as the primary source of data on teaching. The inspection approach to evaluation assumes a constancy of teaching acts and a limit to the teaching repertoire that are not representative of the range of relevant actions and decisions that are central to good teaching.

Evaluators expect to see the teacher presenting a lesson so that they can observe the behaviours listed on the evaluation form. If, in an unscheduled visit, the evaluator finds students working individually or in small groups on assignments, taking a test, or doing something other than listening to the teacher lecture, it is generally agreed that the visit should be rescheduled so that the evaluator can observe the teacher doing things that can be checked off on the form.

Unfortunately, observations of this type reveal little about the coherence of the curriculum, the depth and breadth of content covered, the range of teaching techniques used, the quality and variety of materials employed, the types and frequency of student assignments, the quality of instruments (tests, papers, projects) used for student assessment, the kinds of feedback students receive on their work, or the appropriateness of any of these things for the classroom context. These are all important elements of teaching (even, arguably, more important than the ability to deliver a lecture) that are not attended to in traditional evaluation processes.

Moreover, research shows that not much reliance can be placed on teacher evaluation results based on observation, and few generally valid conclusions can be drawn from them, particularly when low-inference instruments (those that record the frequency of discrete teaching behaviours) are used (Darling-Hammond, Wise and Pease, 1983; Shavelson and Dempsey-Attwood, 1976). The same teacher observed on different occasions will exhibit markedly different teaching behaviours. Teaching acts such as instructional format, pacing, and choice of activities tend to vary with elements of the teaching context (Stodolsky, 1984). Thus, the same elementary teacher will use different approaches to the teaching of mathematics and social studies.

The same secondary teacher will use varied approaches when teaching the same subject matter to different classes of students. Teaching acts vary depending on, among other things, cognitive level of instructional goals, the curriculum structure, and the stage of development of a unit or course of study (e.g. introduction of concepts, practice in performance, reinforcement or skill application).

The current trend toward more widespread use of 'objective', low-inference evaluation instruments - especially prominent where state-developed instruments are mandated - only exacerbates the tendency to think of teaching as an unvarying didactic exercise that is unresponsive to the characteristics of students or the nature of learning tasks. Such instruments are called 'objective' because they require the evaluator only to note whether particular teaching behaviours are present or absent, not whether the actions observed are good or bad, appropriate or inappropriate. They seek to make evaluation - which is and must be an intrinsically subjective and judgmental activity - 'evaluator proof' by reducing the rating process to a tallying exercise requiring no inference or judgment. This is consonant with the bureaucratic approach to evaluation, since the designation of who evaluates is a function of role rather than expertise. Without expertise, judgments cannot be trusted. However, the attempt to make evaluation judgment-free makes it instead trivial and meaningless.

The 'research' cited as the basis for low-inference evaluation instruments is generally a subset of research on teaching that shows that 'direct' instructional techniques predict teacher effectiveness for elementary school students on multiple-choice tests of rudimentary basic skills. 'Direct' instruction consists of teacher-directed activities using sequenced and structured materials that are congruent with tasks on achievement tests and that are administered with constant monitoring of students, using single-answer questions and drill at a low cognitive level (Rosenshine, 1979). However, 'indirect' instructional approaches - such as the use of higher-order, divergent and open-ended questions in student-initiated discourse and development of activities - has been found to support student performance on higher-order tasks as well as student independence and curiosity (see e.g. Peterson, 1979). In addition, teaching behaviour sometimes found to be effective often bears a curvilinear relationship to achievement (Peterson and Kauchak, 1982; Soar, 1972). Obviously, teacher effectiveness is not a monolithic construct.

As an example of this phenomenon, one state has developed an evaluation instrument for teachers that lists a set of context- free teaching behaviours found in 'the research' to predict effectiveness. The behaviours include such things as 'starts class on time' and 'keeps a brisk pace of instruction'. The instrument does not weigh the relative importance of starting class on time, nor does it consider when a brisk pace of instruction is appropriate. It does not allow us to ask whether it is more productive to introduce certain concepts 'briskly' or slowly, whether there are not occasions when student reflection improves absorption, or whether, in sum, this is an appropriate criterion for judging teaching. We would certainly not evaluate doctors on the speed with which they conduct consultations or perform surgery.

The instrument entirely excludes human relations skills or the capacity to communicate with or relate to children because these are not easily measured with objective indicators . It also excludes for the same reason teacher planning and preparation, knowledge of subject matter, the integrity of the curriculum, and a variety of other factors important to good teaching. The most important aspects of teaching are ignored in favour of measuring the measurable , no matter how trivial . This type of standard cannot claim to assess the quality of teaching in a comprehensive way. More important, it cannot serve as a vehicle for improving the teaching practices of the majority of teachers.

Even where more intelligent assessment tools are used, and they are used in good faith by trained evaluators who strive to make time available for evaluation , the effects on overall instructional quality are limited by the design of the bureaucratic evaluation process. Evaluators may be able to identify the grossly incompetent and offer some useful advice to some teachers. But for most teachers the infrequency of evaluation feedback and its generic quality leave most pressing problems of teaching practice untouched. Moreover, because the findings and judgments made in individual evaluations are discussed only between the evaluator and teacher, the outcomes of evaluation do not contribute in a more general way to the articulation and transferal of professional standards of practice.

Bureaucratic schemes of this type exist in the USA largely because administrators and elected representatives demand, on behalf of the community, that teachers are accountable. If they are to avoid the detrimental effects of these schemes, it seems clear that teachers themselves must take responsibility for the quality of their profession. If legislators, administrators and teacher educators are unable to ensure competence (and both theory and experience suggest that they are), then teachers will have to do so themselves.

Peer review and control are the central tenets of professionalism. However, the achievement of such control is not without problems even in highly developed professions. A balance between professional autonomy and public accountability must always be struck. As we seek to envisage how this can occur in teaching, we can profit from the models offered by other professions as well as by their struggles to achieve this balance.

At the core of the definition of a profession is the notion that its members must define and enforce their own standards of practice. As Barber (1965, p.18) puts it, 'An essential attribute of a professional role is autonomy and self-control regarding the development and application of the body of generalised knowledge in which they alone are expert.'

It is not simply because professions lay claim to a body of knowledge that they must exercise self-control. As Boreham (1983) explains, it is the indetermination of that knowledge - its inability to be reduced to rules or prescriptions for practice - that is the most powerful basis for professions' arguments that they must have autonomy from administrative control in determining occupational tasks and functions. Freidson (1973, p. 55) summarises this argument in explaining the organisation of professional tasks through the authority of institutionalised expertise rather than through rational-legal administrative authority: 'Knowledge-based work, the work of ... professionals ... is by its very nature not amenable to mechanisation and rationalisation ... If it is true that management cannot rationalise such work ... then it can only maintain an administrative framework around it.'

The place of judgment and non-standardisable skill in the work of professionals predicts resistance to codification or task determination by outsiders. Control and review of practice and practitioners, it is argued, must be conducted by peers . Members of professions view peer review as essential to developing and maintaining standards because the nature of their work requires both mastery of a body of knowledge and its application in non-routine situations. Those who are competent to evaluate the appropriateness of professional judgments must themselves be highly knowledgeable in the particular area , must be experienced practitioners (because development of sound professional judgment depends on the ability to translate theory into situation-specific actions, an ability that can only be gained through actual practice in diverse situations), and must be familiar with the current state of the art in the particular professional area. Evaluation of professionals by non-peers (those who do not hold the same qualifications) reduces the accuracy and validity of observations and impedes the further development of standards of practice by divorcing practitioners from the standard-setting process.

Moreover, peer review in most professions is thought to be critical to maintaining the special relationship between professionals and their clients. Professionals, as contrasted with other workers, are expected to apply their specialised knowledge in diagnosing a situation and choosing among alternative solution strategies that will benefit the client. The primary responsibility is to do whatever will best serve the client's welfare rather than follow orders from superordinates, implement standardised procedures, or even do what a client himself might propose. As Sykes (1984, p. 3; emphasis added) notes:

> 'What marks a professional's relation to the client is a high degree of trust. We consult physicians, lawyers, and the clergy on matters of the utmost importance and trust their judgment. In turn, the professional is not out to please clients but to do what is best for them. Quacks and charlatans pander to the populace, professionals do not. Their authority rests not only on their proven effectiveness but on a willingness to insist on what they judge is best. This extends to the occupation itself: *professionals must be willing to evaluate other members of the profession to point out ignorance and expose malpractice.* To resist quacks and to transmit professional knowledge and service ideals requires a supporting organisation which helps instill these ideals. Professionals then form a community within the community, one of whose functions is to enforce high expectations.'

Thus, peer review is part of the professional's ethical responsibility to clients and to the profession itself, because it furthers the continual development, transmittal and enforcement of standards of practice. However, peer review as a component of formalised evaluation procedures is but a small part of the professional role. Considering the need for specialised, continually evolving knowledge in professional work, and the special nature of the client relationship, professionals must have a large degree of control over day-to-day technical decisions as well as over policies that shape the organisation, structure and content of work tasks.

Although most current discussion of peer review in teaching centres on a very limited concept (of the use of teachers as evaluators in formal teacher evaluation processes), this is not its only, or even its most important, function as it operates in a profession. *Peer review, broadly defined, includes the various means by which professionals determine the content and structure of their work as well as the qualifications necessary for individuals to claim membership in the profession. It includes peer control over decisions that define acceptable practice as well as peer assessment of individual practitioners.* In fact, after graduation from a professional school, individual practitioners' performances are evaluated by how closely they conform to these peer-determined standards of practice.

Professionals argue that without a fair measure of both individual professional autonomy and collective control over technical features of the work clients will be ill-served. This is because other forms of control, for example, bureaucratic or state controls, can operate only through standardised prescriptions for practice, which cannot take full account of either diverse client needs or new technical or environmental developments that shape appropriate practice (Boreham, 1983). Without professional control over technical decision-making, the concept of peer evaluation lacks a substantive base and becomes merely a procedural issue.

In occupations such as medicine and law that have become professions, practitioners have argued more or less successfully for this control over technical decision making and for limits on governmental or administrative intervention. However, this accomplishment has not come without a struggle. Indeed, new forms of peer review have emerged in most modern professions as a means of combating encroaching regulation of practice by nonprofessionals. The experiences of other professions suggest that:

1. Rigorous training and selection, along with continuing education, are prerequisites for professional control over technical decision making.

2. Professional control over technical decision-making cannot be sustained without the articulation, transmittal and enforcement of standards of practice.

3. Standards of practice and professional accountability cannot be sustained without ongoing peer review of practice and substantial peer control over both the 'production process' and the membership of the profession.

Peer review and responsibility are central to all facets of professional decision making, not just the personnel evaluation process as we generally think of it in teaching. However, teacher involvement in school decision making is currently a relatively haphazard occurrence. Although in some school districts teachers participate in decisions concerning textbook selection, curriculum development, staff development, and other important teaching matters, in others these decisions are made primarily by administrators or school board members. In only a very few schools or districts do teachers have an effective voice in decisions that structure teaching work: decisions about class scheduling, course requirements student placements, programmes, development, or teacher assignments. In even fewer do teachers have any input into personnel decisions concerning the hiring, evaluation, and tenure of either teachers or administrators.

Lack of voice in these matters means that teachers are often expected to practise their profession under conditions that may be administratively convenient but are not especially conducive to effective teaching. Where there is no responsibility for shaping practice, there can be no accountability for appropriate practice, only for following standard operating procedures.

It is important that peer review be considered in this broader context of teacher collaboration in decision-making and participating in problem-solving. The substitution or supplementation of administrators by teachers in traditional evaluation processes in and of itself will do little to change the overall role of teachers in professional decision making. It is the degree to which teachers assume collective responsibility for instructional quality that determines professionalism. Although peer review in formal evaluation processes may be one component of this collective responsibility, peer involvement in decision-making and evaluation of practice must be pervasive if it is to produce a professional concept of teaching.

This is not to argue that no progress is possible until all aspects of school governance are changed. Serious attempts at peer review and involvement, however they are begun, are likely to affect other areas of decision-making as well, as habits of collaboration and consultation take hold and their benefits become apparent. However, it is crucial that the design of teacher evaluation processes that might involve teachers in assessment or assistance of their peers should not replicate the problems that plague existing evaluation procedures. Having teachers without sufficient time, training, or expertise running around with the same old checklists, squeezing in observations of other teachers will not enhance the quality of teacher supervision or improve the opportunities for professional development . Such an approach would be a perversion of the concept of peer review. Credible and legitimate peer review requires different concepts of evaluation than those currently prevailing in most school systems.

Elements of a more productive approach to the evaluation of teaching can be gleaned from practices in other professions as well as practices in school districts that have moved away from traditional bureaucratic conceptions of teaching. I shall describe some promising strategies, fully recognising that variations on these themes may be more appropriate in some contexts, and that there is no one 'right answer' to the problems of improving teaching quality and establishing professional accountability.

The basic elements I propose are based on several principles:

1. Selection and induction into teaching should be rigorous and peer-dominated so that standards of practice can be effectively transmitted and the public can have confidence that teachers are competent.

2. Periodic reviews of individual teachers' performances should be conducted by expert peers and administrators using a wide range of indicators that deal with both the substance and process of teaching. The results of these reviews and of self-evaluation should guide professional development.

3. Special forums and support systems should exist for the referral and redress of apparent cases of malpractice, incompetence, or unprofessional performance.

4. Peer review of teaching practice should be ongoing and include all teachers, so that standards of practice can be continually developed and improved.

5. Teachers should collectively control technical decisions about the structure, form and content of their work.

The examples below illustrate how these principles might be put into practice. They do not represent the sum total of possibilities, nor do they resolve every implementation question that might arise. However, each has the virtue of having been implemented successfully somewhere and thus can lay some claim to feasibility.

Although teacher education and qualification are the initial stages of professional evaluation, they are beyond the purview of school districts and of this chapter. Hiring and tenure are the first evaluative decisions made in an American school district. Though selection and induction are not usually thought of as part of evaluation, the manner in which they are conducted determines the degree of collective professional responsibility for subsequent teacher performance and the extent to which the preconditions for professional decision-making have been met.

East Williston, New York, provides an example of rigorous, teacher-dominated selection practices for both teachers and administrators. When a teaching vacancy is to be filled, the school principal appoints a team made up primarily of teachers who write a job announcement that is then widely advertised. The team screens applications conducts lengthy interviews of short-listed candidates, calls references, and visits their schools to observe the candidates teaching and to gather additional information from teachers and others. When this is not possible, demonstration lessons are scheduled in East Williston. The team then arrives at a recommendation for the superintendent, who personally interviews those on the shortlist.

As a result of this process, new teachers in East Williston are not only viewed as highly competent, they are considered members of the faculty by the faculty themselves. Having participated in the selection process, teachers feel a professional responsibility for the subsequent performance of new colleagues, which reinforces the collegiality that provides a basis for developing and maintaining shared teaching norms and standards . Autonomous performance is expected of teachers in East Williston: the selection process allows faith in the proper use of autonomy and couples it to a sense of collective responsibility for high standards of practice.

A major vehicle for professional preparation and socialisation is the supervised internship or apprenticeship that occurs in most professions during the initial years of practice. It is during these first experiences that a young professional learns how to translate theory into practice, make complex judgments, and (it is hoped) develop a wide repertoire of strategies that will lead to successful decision making. It is also during this period, often before completing probation, that the most intensive evaluation of performance takes place. The presumption is that if candidates cannot demonstrate proficiency at this stage in their careers, they should not continue in the profession.

Toledo, Ohio, has one of the most carefully designed and implemented internship programmes for new teachers. Toledo may be the first school system in the country to institute a truly collaborative approach to the supervision and evaluation of first-year teachers in which peer review plays a central role (Darling-Hammond, 1984).

The intern programme, launched in 1981 at the initiative of the Toledo Federation of Teachers (TFT), places newly hired, inexperienced teachers under the supervision of expert consulting teachers for their initial teaching year. The consulting teachers are released from classroom duties to supervise no more than ten interns in their grade level or subject area. These consultants, chosen by a panel of teachers and administrators for their own exemplary teaching records, are responsible for supervising, assisting, and evaluating the interns in all areas relating to teaching competence. Having observed and consulted with the interns on all aspects of instruction on a weekly basis, the consulting teachers have a comprehensive and well-documented foundation on which to base their evaluative judgments. The principal rates the intern only on non-instructional performance (e.g., attendance and compliance with district policies). In the second probationary year, the principal assumes the conventional supervisory role.

The consulting teachers' recommendations regarding future employment of interns are reported twice annually to the intern review board, a nine-member panel composed of five teacher representatives appointed by the TFT and four administration representatives appointed by the superintendent. The review board carefully reviews the assessments made by consulting teachers, discusses the interns' progress with the consultants at some length and then votes to accept or reject the consultants' individual recommendations, forwarding these determinations to the superintendent for final action. All consulting teachers attend the several meetings each year, which fosters the continuing articulation of standards of practice against which teaching is assessed.

In contrast to previous practice, the contracts of some new teachers are not renewed. As a result of the internship programme, new teachers in Toledo believe they have made great progress in mastering the art of teaching: other teachers and administrators believe that those who are asked to stay in the district are truly competent.

The intern programme is a decided step toward professionalisation of teaching in the Toledo public schools. The central role of peer review by 'master' teachers in the evaluation process is one element of a professional concept of teaching. Another element is the assumption of professional competence underlying an evaluation system that rigorously screens entrants to teaching and is then reactivated only if serious problems become evident later in a teacher's career. Although administrative supervision occurs in the interim (after the probationary period ends principals evaluate teachers once every four years), the system emphasises preparing and screening new teachers so that the need for continuous supervision is minimised. Most important, careful induction of new entrants is an important step toward professionalism. It signals a concern with teaching quality that must be central to client-oriented practice.

As one principal noted, 'Having a joint partnership for evaluation removes a roadblock to action and ultimately benefits kids. Control of entry is a sign of a profession that teaching has never had before ... Consulting teachers provide the time, the subject matter expertise, and good documentation necessary for sound evaluation to occur.'

Although most evaluation processes claim to serve most conceivable purposes, their design allows them to serve only certain purposes well. There are trade-offs involved in each feature of evaluation design. Elements that are intended to heighten reliability tend to reduce the ability of the system to help individual teachers improve, since the uniformity of criteria and their application, which are required for making personnel decisions, necessarily reduce the flexibility that would be needed to make evaluation useful to individual teachers with different needs. Because most school districts' evaluation systems still strive simultaneously to monitor performance against a common standard while professing to promote individual improvement, they are insufficiently sensitive to the teacher's stage of personal and professional development and the context-specific features of the teacher's work to prove very useful for the latter.

If the assumption of competence based on careful selection and induction were met, the presumed need for annual inspections of teacher performance to 'catch' incompetence would be greatly reduced. Evaluative activity could explicitly be aimed at continuing professional development - rather than seeking to assess minimal competence - and could assume the individualistic character most appropriate to this goal. When the goal of evaluation is individual professional development, then self-evaluation and personal goal-setting, along with a review of practice which is relevant to the conditions in which the teacher is working, are the most appropriate strategies. Opportunities for self-assessment and for reference to personal standards of performance strongly influence self-efficacy and motivation. Goal-setting is based on a view of desired practice, which requires knowledge of alternatives to current practice, and on a careful consideration of current practice through self-evaluation.

To accomplish this, Barber (1984) proposed a 'peer-mediated self-appraisal' approach to evaluation solely for the purpose of individual improvement. Under this system, tenured teachers would be professionally obliged to undergo self-evaluation annually and to use peer review periodically. As part of self- evaluation, teachers could use data from any source - student achievement, personal reflection on practice, observations from parents or administrators - to make judgments about their own teaching and to set goals for the coming year.

One model of such a goal-setting process operates at Greenwich, Connecticut (Wise et al., 1984). Teachers in Greenwich annually set individual goals for evaluation, along with plans for achieving the goals and means for assessing the extent to which the goals have been accomplished. Personally appropriate professional development strategies, such as observation of other teachers, coursework, workshop attendance, or readings may be part of the plan. This process is conducted in conjunction with an evaluator, who may be a principal or a teacher leader. Although system-wide goals may be chosen, the evaluation process allows for individualised definitions of growth and development rather than standardised definitions that ignore a teacher's particular teaching context or personal stage of growth. At the end of the year, both the teacher and the evaluator write a narrative assessment of progress toward the goals so established. Goals may be 'recycled' for the subsequent year or new goals may be established.

In Barber's model, a committee of peers would serve as the referent for self-evaluation. Such a committee, comprised mostly of teachers in the same or a related teaching area as the individual teacher, would be selected and convened every few years by the career teacher. The composition of the committee might be subject to approval by the principal or department head. Following the better practices of some higher education institutions, the committee would provide a review of teaching practices through an examination of such documents as lesson plans, examinations, examples of graded assignments, course materials and classroom observations. This process would cover a broad spectrum of performance, encompassing not only performance in the classroom but also intentionality (what the teacher intends to have happen) and other teaching behaviour as exhibited by assignments and grading practices. The assumption underlying this approach is that peers who are familiar with the classroom environment, subject matter, and demands on a teacher can best render specific and practical suggestions for improvement.

In addition, in Barber's conception, 'teachers own the evaluation strategy and the results of self-evaluation or peer review. Inservice training provides teachers with the information, skills and techniques to use peer review information to individualise and improve their teaching. Training is provided by a board made up solely of teachers and held in teacher centres' (Barber, 1984, p. 8).

Perhaps most important, the process would give all teachers the opportunity to assess themselves and others, to begin to develop a consensus about good practice, and to link evaluation to their professional development activities. As discussed below, this process would be buttressed by continuing peer review of policy and practice. Its formative character would be safeguarded by the existence of alternative avenues for addressing the infrequent but important problems of experienced teachers who have extreme difficulty in maintaining professional standards of practice.

Every school district contains some small number of teachers who, because of personal problems or teaching incompetence, fail to provide even minimally adequate instruction to students or are even abusive to the children they are supposed to serve. Most teacher evaluation systems are notably ineffective in gaining help for these teachers or removing them from classrooms. Typically, both unions and administrators 'play ostrich' while these teachers are transferred from one school to another, because neither the will nor the resources are present to assist them or terminate their employment.

In a world where selection and induction into teaching are serious and careful undertakings, the number of teachers who encounter these kinds of difficulties should be exceedingly small. But it is extremely important that a formal mechanism exist for referral, assistance and decision making in such cases. Such a mechanism can ensure that procedures are fair, supports are adequate and truly intensive assistance is offered while the welfare of students is protected and professionalism is also advanced.

An example is given below of evaluation programmes within which such teachers receive assistance from their peers. Teachers alone do not make a final determination about the continued employment of the teacher they have assisted. However, where teacher organisations have collaborated with administrators in designing and implementing programmes to address these situations, they provide the kind of process and assistance that are necessary for both improvement and personnel decision-making.

The intervention programme in Toledo uses the same cadre of consulting teachers who work with interns to supervise experienced teachers who are having difficulty in the classroom. Candidates for intervention assistance are recommended by both teacher representatives on the union's building committee and the principal. Once placed in the programme, the intervention teacher receives intensive supervision and assistance from an assigned consulting teacher in the same teaching area who, though not ultimately responsible for evaluation, makes recommendations about when intervention assistance should end, either because the teacher has improved sufficiently or because further assistance would not be productive. The intern review panel (described earlier) recommends termination or reinstatement on a provisional or permanent basis to the superintendent, based on the report of the consulting teacher and additional data as needed.

In Toledo about half of the teachers needing intervention or remedial supervision have left teaching; the remainder improved sufficiently to be reinstated. Although the professional organisations will provide legal assistance to a teacher who wishes to fight a termination decision, this rarely occurs because opportunities for improvement have been provided. The impediments to professional accountability are reduced through the introduction of professional involvement and responsibility (Wise et al., 1984).

What I have described above are means for evaluating teachers at different career stages and in various circumstances. By differentiating the purposes and methods of evaluation and by involving peers in the evaluation process, I believe the multiple goals of evaluation can be more effectively and efficiently served. These kinds of evaluation processes are important for establishing professional accountability in teaching. However, there is another evaluative function rarely performed in schools which, as we have seen, is central to the operation of other professional organisations. That function is a continuous review of practice by professionals who also play a major role in establishing the policies which, in large measure, determine practice.

This evaluative function serves the joint purposes of monitoring organisational activities and establishing a continuous dialogue about problems of practice among the practitioners themselves. The very distant equivalent in school systems is programme evaluation, an activity generally conducted by central office researchers who report findings to government sponsors and school board members. Teachers are neither the major producers nor consumers of such information. Hence, as we have learned from research on implementation and change, neither they nor their students are the major beneficiaries of such evaluation results.

Teachers need to discuss immediate, concrete problems of teaching practice on a regular basis if teaching theory is ever to be transformed into meaningful standards of practice. Reducing teacher isolation and establishing dialogue will require providing time during the school day for teachers to observe one another teach and to meet in order to talk about what they are doing and why they are doing it.

An investment of even two hours per week for all teachers could have a substantial influence on teachers' knowledge, opportunities for reflection and motivation. What is critical is that teachers have both time to pursue such activities as part of their role (rather than as 'release' or extracurricular time) and authority to make changes based on their collective discoveries.

A glimpse of what is possible is offered in the effective schools literature, which has discovered that participatory school management by teachers, based on collaborative planning, collegial problem solving, and constant intellectual sharing, can produce both student learning gains and increased teacher satisfaction and retention (Mackenzie, 1983; Pratzner, 1984). Though teachers in these settings may or may not be involved in direct peer review for formal evaluation purposes, they none the less practise a form of evaluation and peer review when they identify problems, observe one another share ideas, and ask, 'How are we doing?' The enquiry ethic that permeates these schools improves standards of practice by decreasing teacher isolation and providing directly relevant opportunities for professional growth.

Salt Lake City offers one example of teacher participation and empowerment in professional decision making. Teachers in Salt Lake City exercise considerable power over teaching decisions through the teacher evaluation system and the 'shared governance' approach to school administration. Codified in Article XIV of the Salt Lake Teachers' Association (SLTA) contract, shared governance delegates authority in many school matters to both teachers and parents. The agreement provides for the president and executive director of the SLTA to attend all of the superintendent's staff meetings, for the joint development of preliminary budget proposals with management, and for the parity vote of teachers on school committees dealing with class size, teaching load, teacher assignments, in-service policy and the allocation of funds for travel and conventions, elementary report card policy (shared with parents), and the filling of administrative vacancies.

Furthermore, the superintendent's strong conviction that teachers should never have surrendered control over curriculum decisions has led to a cadre of 40 teacher specialists who receive small stipends and some release time to serve as curriculum leaders . Jointly chosen by management and the SLTA, they provide curricular expertise to both teachers and central office learning specialists who organise and serve on remedial teams. Other teachers may call on teacher specialists for instructional advice, and the specialists, along with other teachers, conduct in-service workshops. Teachers are responsible for curriculum development and articulation at the school level; the support they need is provided by their peers.

Professional development and accountability through peer review are the central means for defining, transmitting and enforcing standards of practice in a profession. Viewed broadly, peer review encompasses activities ranging from the training, qualification, hiring, and induction of new entrants, to continuing dialogue on problems of professional practice and collegially defined professional development, as well as participation in formalised evaluation processes.

Peer review can take many forms, with varying degrees of involvement and responsibility for assessment and assistance. Although in teaching peer review may currently be seen as undermining management 'rights' or union strength, in practice it could improve the accuracy, fairness and relevance of evaluation and staff development activities with commensurate gains for administrators, teachers and, most important, students. Judiciously applied models of peer review could extend teachers' control over both the conditions of teaching and the quality of instruction, simultaneously upgrading standards of practice and the status of the profession.

In the long run, efforts to enhance professional accountability, if they involve teachers as full partners, can bolster the authority and control of teachers over the substance and conduct of their profession. On the other hand, failure to deal with the problems of teacher supervision will lead only to increased bureaucratic controls over education and the further de-professionalisation of teaching.

Policy makers and educators must collectively find ways to make visible improvements to the methods for defining who becomes a teacher and for creating standards of teaching practice. Peer review is an important initial step toward a true teaching profession.

Chapter 10

Preparation and Training to Support Appraisal

Andy Smith

The philosophy and approach explored in this chapter have an unashamedly experiential base: the academic rationale and its historical development have been left to others. The focus of the chapter contains the practicalities of developing appraisal from scratch, training the various groups involved and the ongoing training demands likely to result from the appraisal process itself. While the general demands anticipated as a result of the introduction of an appraisal scheme across a body of 400,000 professional teachers in three to four years are considered, particular attention will be given to the training support required at three specific levels: local education authorities, schools and teachers.

Experiential base

The approach to the training models detailed here rests upon three foundations. First, it rests upon experience gained over the last ten years of leading teachers in exploring concepts of their own personal and professional development. Appraisal extends this work, offers a structured approach and a right of access to this structure to every teacher. It also goes some way towards securing resources to meet some of the identified personal and professional development needs.

Second, I am concerned about the process through which an understanding of the content and the methodology of appraisal is achieved. My commitment is always to involve people actively in their own learning, as training involves managing the learning of others rather than simply teaching them. I have often called attention to the importance of matching the process of learning to the content that is being explored. While there is room for debate about how much active involvement benefits certain areas of understanding, when the learning is about the skills and concepts involved in appraisal an 'active' approach is the best match of process to content.

The third source for the principles and practice of training that I am about to outline is my own experience over the last three years. I have designed and led the training for headteacher and schoolteacher appraisal in two of the six DES pilot authorities and I am at present consultant trainer to 18 other authorities. While what follows cannot claim to be a perfect approach, it is certainly based on sufficient practice to form a useful starting point for others who are looking for guidelines. It is a description of the preparation and training that should be undertaken within a local education authority, then within the schools and finally covers the concerns of individual teachers and headteachers.

Managing one change against a matrix of other changes

A common and sometimes justified criticism of trainers within the current educational scene is that they appear oblivious to the complex set of competing pressures bearing on local authorities, schools and individual teachers.

The first concern in looking at the preparation and training for the introduction of appraisal must be the context within which appraisal across the teaching profession is to take place. Nothing takes place in isolation and appraisal is interwoven with the three other major legislative changes that are to affect the education process in schools over the next three or four years.

The introduction of the national curriculum, testing and assessment, and the local management of schools are all current legislative changes. It would be nice to think that each of these developments was supported by a well worked through developmental plan within each authority and that the combination of each of these developmental plans was co-ordinated within a larger strategic plan. The introduction of appraisal, touching as it does every teacher, presents a strong case for a re-examination of this position.

The concern of anybody managing such an overall strategic plan should be that the loading on schools and individuals in schools who are affected by these changes should be as evenly spread as is humanly possible.

I am not suggesting that one can turn round and say 'we will do National Curriculum this year and will introduce appraisal next year'. It should, however, not be beyond the imagination of educational planners within authorities to spread the load. Trainers designing implementation programmes for appraisal need to demonstrate this.

It is very important that the preparation and training that supports the introduction of any one of these, and my concern here is for appraisal, both recognises the load coming from the other directions and provides the managers of appraisal with some strategies for working with the managers of the other three.

I am quite convinced that if 'managers' fail to filter the demands associated with each of these legislative changes and schools are asked to cope unnecessarily with too much in any one of the coming five years then the result will be the 'burn out' of senior staff, alienation from the ideas and a breakdown in the personal relationships that are the foundation stone on which successful change in education is dependent. We are now in a situation where the funding base for these legislative changes is predictable over at least three years; the development plans should therefore not be too difficult to draw up.

Appraisal is dependent on a certain climate of opinion within an organisation and that climate itself is often dependent on the organisation's ability to manage a number of changes at once. As the project leaders of each of these legislative changes slowly become more committed to the success of their own ventures they often lose sight of the impact they are having on other areas. They still, however, recognise the impact that the other changes are having on them.

A starting point for any local authority in the introduction of appraisal is a development plan extending over at least three years, maybe more if necessary. This development plan should be overlaid on the other existing or emerging development plans designed to support the other changes.

A senior officer should be given the responsibility of making sure that the people (usually project leaders) within the local authority responsible for heading the development of the national curriculum, local management of schools, testing and assessment and appraisal have a concern for the health of the education service as a whole while supporting their own individual enterprises.

When one considers the training strategies and the training of trainers to support these ventures, many of the skills, such as managing adult learning, are generic to all of them. It is not uncommon (as well as being economic) for a senior officer to co-ordinate the operation of these trainers across more than one field.

The following therefore rests on the assumption that within the local authority the development plan to support appraisal sits alongside three other development plans. As a whole, the four are combined into a strategic plan for the management of legislative change within that authority.

What follows is concerned specifically with appraisal. It outlines the stages a trainer must take each group through as appraisal is introduced. For example, all parties from the local authority steering group or working party through to each teacher in school must have firm grasp of the philosophical base for appraisal in that authority.

A philosophical base

The successful introduction of appraisal requires a sound philosophical base which is understood and shared by the policy makers. This enables the trainers to structure and deliver their courses with a clear understanding of the intention behind the process. It affects the processes that are used, the vocabulary that is selected and the outcomes that are perceived by all of the participants. It is an area that must be given a considerable amount of attention at the beginning of any preparation and training course.

There are a number of different approaches to exploring a philosophical base. I have outlined one below which was developed originally by Vennassa Champion (now appraisal co-ordinator for Cumbria) and myself in an attempt to explain to others the roots of that particular pilot. It leans on the concept of continua to describe the relative positions of the issues involved. This is a particularly useful way either for a local authority to explore where it stands or for teachers within a local authority to identify where the local authority's starting point actually is.

The table below represents a list of the different positions that people have been seen to take when considering appraisal.

What is your philosophical position?

Accountability..Professional Development

Incompetence..Competence

Hierarchical..Professional Partnership

Looking at the past......................................Looking to the future

Hearsay...Shared experience

Suspicion...Trust

- .... Appraisee involvement in structure and process .... +

- .... Appraisee's access to information .... +

Professional development

This illustrates the classic debate. Are we talking about an accountability model or a professional development model? The National Steering Group, on which all parties were represented, has come down unequivocally in favour of a professional development model (DES 1989). This was the starting point outlined by ACAS, it was supported by the six pilots and, once understood by teachers, was warmly embraced.

These two positions are often presented as mutually exclusive and, while they can produce radically different schemes, it is also possible from one starting point to achieve a fair measure of both. I firmly believe that, while a rigorous approach to a professional development model will, alongside staff development outcomes, ensure a measure of accountability, I can see no such side effects from an accountability model. *The training process* must make people aware of this distinction. A trainer also needs to understand the recent developments in commerce and industry. Here, moves from models of accountability to professional development have been introduced - and from a profit motive.

Competence

Often stated, but not essentially connected with the previous continua, is the idea that appraisal is about identifying the incompetent performer. But the distinction is quite clear; appraisal assumes that the teacher is competent. The aim of the appraisal process is to recognise and record that competence and to identify and provide support to help develop further a teacher's skills. That is not say that on occasion two teachers involved in the appraisal process might not find themselves concerned that one of them is not competent. Again, it is a matter of intention. The appraisal process is not there to confirm this: other procedures are available within the authority and the training process must identify for appraisers how they suspend the appraisal process and identify support for a member of staff with problems.

Professional partnership

The quality of the relationship between the appraisee and the appraiser is all important. No amount of careful structuring of an appraisal process will allow an appraisee to benefit from a relationship with an appraiser who is not respected. It will be the norm for the appraiser to be a senior colleague, usually educations's version of the 'line manger'. It should still be possible, if both teachers understand the potential of appraisal, for the process to be conducted within the context of a professional partnership. The training process should ensure this. A discussion, especially amongst appraisers, will soon establish where their view of appraisal would sit on the above continuum. A trainer's concern in this area is often explaining to an appraiser how an understanding of this relationship is conveyed. It is easily misunderstood by an appraisee.

Looking to the future through a shared experience

Appraisal will change in nature as experience, confidence and competence build up. As we start out, it is important to some extent to displace the previous understanding of each other's work unless it is both very recent and was gained from first hand shared experience. Appraisers do not operate on second hand information, no matter how current. A teacher's work is viewed with the teacher. Looking ahead from a shared experience is a sound base to build upon. Shared experience is just what it says, it produces a dynamic between two people that is unique. When involved in appraisal on second and subsequent occasions, reflecting on previous shared experience may well be appropriate. A major component of the training process will be a concentration on this element, variously termed classroom observation, task observation, teaching analysis or looking at learning.

Trust

A conclusion reached on every training course that I have been involved with suggests that trust is the most essential component of the whole procedure. It is usually achieved through an understanding of what exactly is going to happen and the control that the appraisee has over both the content and the process. It is also closely connected to the existing climate within the school staff. It follows then that the training process will need to address the development of an appropriate climate within a school before the introduction of appraisal. A bad start to appraisal can be very expensive in terms of personal relationships; if in doubt, I would advise starting with 'whole school' review and deferring appraisal.

Appraisee involvement and access to information

Two final guides follow that enable one to discuss the nature of the appraisal process that is being suggested. Appraisees, for all sorts of reasons, usually interpret appraisal as the province of senior management. This view needs to be dispelled. The training process should involve both appraisees and appraisers in the development of the structure of appraisal in a school. This, together with total access to all the information recorded with the appraisal procedure, will contribute to the confidence of all.

All of the above deserve substantial discussion. Such a discussion preceded by a formal input illustrating each point would be best conducted in small groups. This would form the first stage in the preparation for appraisal.

It is important to point out that one would not seek the same position on each of the continua but I would be disturbed if it were to drift too far to the left of centre on the continuum diagram set out on page 164.

Trainers also need to be alert to a number of other issues that surface to a greater or lesser extent. Sharing these concerns with participants early on and agreeing a way of tackling them will be well rewarded.

Two definitions should therefore guide training strategies.

- APPRAISAL: A structured approach to staff development with the individual as its starting point.
- THE APPRAISAL PROCESS: One professional holding himself/herself accountable to himself/herself in the presence of another professional.

Preparing the ground

The preparation stage that precedes training is very important and can be crucial to the success of the training strategies and their implementation.

The whole concept of appraisal is surrounded by misinterpretation and a good deal of mythology. One of the essential tasks to be tackled when introducing appraisal within a local authority is the construction of a very clear statement on how the local authority views appraisal. Ideally, this local authority policy statement will be written in collaboration with all the relevant parties, including representatives of schools involved, professional associations, representatives of the advisers and officers of the local authority and elected members. The language used in this statement should be very carefully considered; it is to be hoped that the local authority will be leaning towards a professional development model of appraisal and the way it describes its model should leave this in no doubt. People will focus on all sorts of cues to confirm their fears.

It is also helpful if the professional associations make a separate statement to their members within each local authority about how they view the local authority's statement. In my experience a trainer is going to be confronted with this anyway so it is as well for it to be sorted out at the beginning. On training courses teachers quite often (and quite rightly) ask about the local professional associations' view of this particular development and giving sensible and accurate reassurance is very important.

The next two stages go hand in hand; first, the local authority needs to develop a structured plan for the introduction of appraisal and, second, a training strategy that will actually support this.

The descriptions should contain 'accurate information'. By this I mean that they should include information about all the stages to do with appraisal - the documentation, the vocabulary that is going to be used to describe the various stages within the appraisal cycle, the appeals procedure. There is nothing so disconcerting as having to change terminology or the documentation used once a number of schools within the authority have their schemes up and running. It might be quite acceptable within pilot studies, working with the good will of all the teachers involved, but when extending the appraisal scheme to all teachers, such small changes chip away at the credibility of the training process. To expect teachers to introduce appraisal in the absence of some hard and fast guidelines on, for example, an appeals procedure, would be to court disaster.

As one disseminates the local authority policy statement, the view of the professional associations and a structure plan for the introduction of appraisal, it is very important to give people clear descriptions of what will happen at each stage. This has been successfully done at a number of awareness day courses using different approaches, including training videos.

Finally, it is important for a trainer to remember that appraisal provides an opportunity for every teacher to take a structured approach to their own professional development. It is not a process which will force them to do this.

Types and patterns of preparation and training

Having developed the policy statement, there is a natural progression through which the local authority structure plan will proceed towards the introduction of appraisal.

First and foremost, as with any education change (especially one of this magnitude) and despite the advice obtained from the national pilot studies and from the evaluation report, a local authority would be wise to start with a small pilot of its own. This enables the authority to build on current experience and develop an approach that fits its own culture. It is from within the experience of its own small pilot that the authority will identify and train a cadre of trainers.

Experienced trainers are going to be needed for some time, first to support development of appraisal within the authority which in itself is going to be a major task, and second, to meet the training demands associated with appraisal that will continue to surface as appraisal becomes part of normal professional life. This latter demand should, over four to five years, find its place in the normal staff development programmes for senior management within education.

Although it is not appropriate here to list the details of each training programme (there are just too many variants), it is possible to describe both the type of training programmes that need to be constructed and the issues that should be tackled in each of them.

The training sequence following a published and agreed policy would address the following:

Awareness raising

- Headteachers
- 'Whole school' review policies
- Principles and practice of appraisal

Skills training

- Associate trainers
- Managers of appraisal
- Appraisees - teachers and headteachers
- Appraisers - teachers, headteachers and inspectors
- Trainers

Awareness raising

Headteachers

I am convinced that the gatekeepers to appraisal within the education service are the headteachers. As with any other education innovation, if people within an institution are not quite clear about what is supposed to happen (whether they agree with it or not), then the development has little chance of success. Headteachers within an authority need to be alerted very early on to the policy and the methods that are going to be used for introducing appraisal within the authority. This is best done at either a headteachers' conference established specifically for this purpose or within the smaller headteachers' meetings that occur throughout the year. This day or session has to be very competently led by somebody who both understands appraisal in detail and has a fairly clear idea of how it is going to be interpreted within the authority. Headteachers are more aware than anybody of the difficulties this may precipitate within their schools, to say nothing of the concern that they may feel over headteacher appraisal. The questions that these sessions give rise to can be very searching.

It would be unwise to hold such meetings until one has thought the scheme through fairly thoroughly. Headteachers usually welcome some advice (this might include the provision of some materials) in presenting this information to the staff within their schools. It is hopes that every teacher would have had a direct letter from the authority about appraisal and the headteacher would be able to build on this. It is normal practice when an employer introduces a fundamental change for all of its employees that they are given individual and detailed notification.

The meeting for the headteachers should ideally be chaired by somebody who can clearly demonstrate the authority's commitment to the process that they are trying to introduce.

'Whole school' review

One of the features of introducing appraisal that has been developed from the work conducted by the national pilot studies is the association between individual appraisal and 'whole school' review, initiated by Cumbria long before it was taken up by any of the other pilot studies.

This again follows one of the principles of successful educational innovation although it is occasionally challenged in industry. The principle suggests that it does not make a lot of sense for two people to sit down and consider how one of them is contributing to the aims and objectives of the institution if the aims and objectives of the institution are not reasonably well understood. Work within the pilot schools suggests that within some schools and colleges the aims and objectives are not clearly understood and have never been discussed in detail. Recent legislation, not least to do with the national curriculum and the involvement of governors, is slowly correcting this balance.

There are a number of different approaches to whole school review. The two principle ones that I have seen operate successfully are Guidelines for Review and Internal Development in Schools (GRIDS) supported by the SCDC and now published by Longman and the approach designed by the International Movement for Educational Change (IMTEC) produced by a Norwegian educational consultant and supported in this country by the National Foundation for Educational Research.

Both approaches move towards the same goal but take radically different routes, although they both start with questionnaires. GRIDS is essentially a developmental process, takes quite a lot of time and by nature of its process involves all teachers in what is going on. IMTEC, however, can be implemented fairly quickly, it also includes all teachers in contributing their ideas to what is going on but it does not actually involve them in a discussion. My experience of both approaches in many different schools indicates that GRIDS has been much more difficult to manage in secondary schools than IMTEC, while IMTEC is limited by the fact that it relies on a snapshot of teachers' experience (the moment they fill in the questionnaire) and that interpretation of some of the questions is rather difficult.

However, both approaches (and there are numerous other home-grown approaches which are also worth considering) involve a roughly similar process. They establish a climate and legitimise within a school or college the practice of reflecting on what is going on and whether or not people are satisfied with it. This then provides a backcloth against which people can discuss their own contribution to and feelings about what is going on.

An interesting development from this has been the suggestion that if 'whole school' review is a useful backdrop against which teachers can consider their contribution to a school's aims and values, a local authority review and clear statement about its policies would form a useful backdrop for headteacher appraisal. It is difficult to imagine how a headteacher can lead (leadership might well be a focus for headteacher appraisal) a school toward the implementation of local policies in all sorts of areas if they do not have clear guidance on these from a local authority that has recently reviewed and published what it believes it is about.

Perhaps as the role of local authorities changes this will become less of a supportable proposition. As reform of the educational system continues, it is to be hoped that 'whole school' review as well as appraisal will become part of normal professional practice; this should result in the development of job descriptions, especially for senior managers within schools, actually to support both of these components.

Principles and practice of appraisal

Introducing the concept of appraisal, the principles on which is to be based and the practice by which it is to be introduced will normally form the first involved discussion that teachers would find themselves in after being notified by both the local authority and the headteacher that appraisal is to take place. Such a discussion is best led by experienced teachers (who are often called associate trainers) from within the local authority. It is a particularly important day. The views that are first gained about appraisal from this source are those that will colour all that follows. The associate trainers need to be well prepared and the day programme carefully planned. If the management of the day attracts the same criticism that surrounds many of the current INSET days delivered in schools the trainers are in for a rough ride. The main components of the day will be: background philosophy, national and local structure, cycle of appraisal, documentation, resource support and training programme. The structure of the day must involve teachers; this is not the place for a didactic approach.

Skills training

Associate trainers

Given the large number of teachers within an authority that has to be introduced to appraisal, a fairly substantial number of associate trainers is going to be needed to enable the introduction to be completed over a period of three to four years. Appraisal is not a process that is easily transmitted by a straight, didactic talk. It requires a balance of information providing small group discussion, illustration skills practice and question and answer. These people will be best drawn from those who have already gained some experience themselves of he process through the authority's early pilot.

Associate trainers will need to cover both the preparation days on the principles of practice of appraisal and the principles and practice of 'whole school' review. For some schools, by the time appraisal is considered, 'whole school' review might well have already been introduced. It is now often used to develop a school national curriculum plan.

The skill that associate trainers value most is the subtle but important distinction between presenting and managing learning for adults rather than for the young people with whom they normally work. Given that appraisal is a fairly challenging and emotive area, getting this subtle distinction wrong can be very expensive in terms of the progress one will subsequently make. It is also important that across an authority the same message is given about the authority's intentions and the way the process is to be managed and supported. This argues that the associate trainers should be developed as a team and should be occasionally brought together to share their experience of teacher reaction across the authority.

Management of appraisal

This is an area to which the DES pilot studies did not give a lot of attention; most of the management and all of the trouble shooting was provided by the project teams. This is quite normal for a developmental pilot but as the scheme extends across every school this function must, for teachers, be accepted by the schools themselves while, for headteachers, this responsibility will always remain with the authority.

The managers of appraisal are going to fall into three broad areas. First, they are going to be the managers of appraisal within schools and experience within the pilots suggests that somebody other than the headteacher should be identified as the manager/co-ordinator of appraisal within a school. One would then refer to the co-ordinator if concerned about a particular appraisal and to the headteacher if concerned about the way appraisal was being managed in the school.

Second, there is the management of headteacher appraisal. The manager of the appraisal process for headteachers has an even more demanding role. Not only are there large numbers when compared with an individual school's staff, but they do not know each other. This presents a very different dynamic. If the DES guidelines are followed there will usually be three people involved instead of two. The geography of the authority can also be a challenge in itself.

Third, there is the management of appraisal across the authority which will include supporting both the individual school co-ordinators and the co-ordinators of the appraisal process for the authority's headteachers.

For both of these groups of people, headteachers across an authority and teachers within a school, there are two areas within the management of appraisal that will need to be considered quite carefully. Firs, there will be the moderation of the quality of what is going on to make certain that not only does every teacher gain their right to appraisal but that they gain the right to the same sensitive and professional approach to appraisal as every other teacher within the school or the authority. Given the numbers involved and the confidentiality that surrounds the process, this is not an easy task.

Second, and some thought has been given to this, there are the logistics of managing all the parts of the process for each teacher and for all the teachers within a school or across a local authority. For example, in a primary school with 10 teachers who are to be appraised every two years, five teachers will be going through the process each year. For a primary school already working under pressure, to include one teacher appraisal every term will not be achieved without help. For the medium size secondary school with 60 staff the logistics become a serious matter. With 30 working weeks (writing off the first and last week of term and the one or two other weeks that it will prove impossible to use), the manager of appraisal in such a school will be tracking the appraisal of one teacher every week of the year.

If the same logic is developed for headteachers across an authority, greater challenges arise. I am currently working with one authority that has 500 institutions and headteachers. Working on the same 30 week formula, we are looking for a plan than can manage the appraisal of 250 headteachers each year; eight a week, or just over one a day, which is a very interesting challenge.

The process for both teachers and headteachers involves an initial meeting, a number of classroom or task observations, an appraisal interview, the writing and agreeing of an appraisal statement and support or follow-up review meetings over the following two years. Given this process, one can start to appreciate the amount of organisation required to ensure that this can be conducted as part of normal professional practice and not be disruptive of the children's learning, which it is hoped it will ultimately enhance.

The training demands for the teachers and officers who are to manage this are substantial. They require a comprehensive understanding of each element of the process and a vision of good practice. They will need the support of management training and contacts with other facing similar challenges.

On the shoulders of these teachers and officers will rest the responsibility of making sure that all their colleagues are similarly treated across the authority and that the money the authority has to support the INSET demands that are identified as a result of this process is fairly distributed and easily accessible. The bottom line for the credibility of appraisal is actually delivering the support at the end of the process. Careful thought will have to be give to securing this. Training and continuous support for the managers of appraisal within schools and the managers of appraisal across an authority will have to become a regular feature.

Appraisees

Preparation and training for appraisees is now accepted as a necessary event, although at some of the initial discussions, while considerable attention was given to the preparation of appraisers, appraisees were often forgotten. Appraisees need help and support in different ways. Some of us, as a result of training in other domains, are quite articulate and confident in talking about ourselves, our strengths and our weaknesses; other find that very difficult.

In my experience, when people find it difficult to talk about themselves, the first area in which they gain confidence is in talking about their weaknesses. This can result in a very unbalanced reflection on their ability. A sensitive introduction to the concept of self review through training is essential.

One of the main learning events of careful appraisee preparation is a switch away from feeling the subordinate partner in the process and a recognition of the demands on an appraiser. This usually gives appraisees considerable confidence but it can only be achieved by immersing them in the process and then taking a look at it.

A useful approach and one of the easiest ways to give appraisees confidence in the appraisal process is to allow them, for a short while, to adopt the position of appraisers. This usually convinces them quite quickly that the appraiser has quite a demanding job. It also prompts the suggestion that appraisers need to be properly prepared for their task and legitimises further training for appraisers. To abstract appraisers for training before appraisees have understood this breeds both resistance and promotes misunderstanding. It is usually quite easily achieved. Everybody, after all, is to be an appraisee at some stage so why not take that as the starting point?

Appraisers

Training for appraisers naturally involves them in looking at both sides of the appraisee/appraiser equation. All appraisers will be appraisees within the process; however, they have the additional responsibility of helping a number of people identify their own professional needs. This is going to require them to lean on different skills and a trainer needs to remember that many people are going to be put in the position of appraisers for reasons other than that they are 'natural' appraisers. They just happen to be a head of department or curriculum leader.

A hallmark of the education profession has always been that when one has demonstrated competence in one area one often gains promotion into another area, usually without training. The conclusion of this development is quite frightening. For appraisal it results in appraisers feeling very insecure. Added to this, they realise that the likely result of getting this role wrong is not just an organisational foul-up but it could also damage personal relationships and an individual's self esteem.

Areas in which appraisers have demonstrated a lack of confidence are: classroom observation, managing the appraisal interview with difficult people (and there are difficult people who are honestly trying to get the most out of the process) and the writing of the agreed statement. All of

these areas need to feature very heavily in a training programme for appraisers.

Trainers

As a consultant trainer I obviously have some fairly strong views in this particular area. Trainers working with experienced teachers need a great deal
more support than they are currently given. The jump between managing
learning for young people and managing learning for adults is a much larger
gap than is popularly imagined.

Trainers need support in three areas. First and the most obvious, they actually need to know the content of what they are talking about. In the same
way as you would not expect someone who had just passed their own 'A'
Level in mathematics to be coaching somebody else up to that level; trainers actually need to know the content in considerable depth. Second, the
training process has to be one of active learning; experience in managing
active learning is a necessary pre-requisite to training in this area. Addition-
ally, appraisal in challenging people's self-esteem and professional identity
is likely to produce discussion and comment that requires extremely sensitive handling. Such skills do not come easily.

Finally, the management of a training course and the way that management is perceived unfortunately always reflects on the way the content of
the course is actually considered by the participants. In truth there is usually
quite a strong connection. The management of courses on appraisal needs
to be absolutely first class. Trainers need support in the way they design
courses, their material should be professionally produced and they should
have continuing feedback on their performance. The training of trainers will
be an important investment for the successful implementation of appraisal.
It does not happen overnight!

In addition, I am quite convinced that the process of appraisal will develop very quickly over the next three years. Trainers will need to come
together to think how their methods of presentation and the way they involve people in exploring the concepts of appraisal can continually develop
to keep pace with people's understanding and interpretation of what is going
on. There is already a body of experience that suggests that when appraisees and appraisers come together for the second time they both have a
much clearer understanding of what they wish to gain from this process and
tackle it in a different way. They are also able to identify the areas in which
they require further training. These gaps will become apparent as appraisers conduct their second set of appraisals. Trainers need to keep abreast
of these feelings and be able to support these new demands.

The future for training

This summary of the various concerns of those with a responsibility for the training to support the preparation and implementation of appraisal only scratches the surface. The detailed specific training programmes to support the components, setting up the system, self review, information collection, classroom or task observation, conducting an appraisal interview and writing an agreed statement, while well developed, are beyond the scope of this chapter.

Although all the above is based on actual experience it is an experience within a particular educational environment. That environment is constantly changing. I am convinced that, as the other legislative changes mentioned at the beginning of this chapter start to take root, they will slowly find their way into the appraisal process. We will need to take care that they are introduced in an acceptable form. The national curriculum, testing and assessment and local management invite any naive practitioner involved with appraisal to slip from professional development to accountability with almost sleight of hand.

As we search for and develop models for training we must also be cautious about where we look. Counselling skills, for example, may be required as an outcome of appraisal: they are not central to the process. Industrial models that link pay to the outcomes of appraisal design different training models to achieve different outcomes. Educational appraisal systems, designed against rather than within culture, North America for example, like some wines do not travel well.

In short, there is no easy solution. We will have to work up our training strategies through experience. I am, however, convinced that from the limited work we have done to date, an experiential approach will ultimately be the most successful.

Recommendations of the National Steering Group

Summary by the DES

1. Appraisal should be introduced within a national framework, comprising Regulations and guidance in the form of a DES Circular.

2. Responsibility for implementing appraisal should rest with LEAs, for all LEA maintained schools including voluntary aided schools. In the case of grant maintained schools the responsibility should rest with governing bodies.

3. The aims of appraisal should be those set out in the 1986 ACAS report - extract attached. They should be set out in the Regulations.

4. Appraisal should respect and promote equal opportunities.

5. Regulations should require LEAs to implement appraisal for all staff on teachers' conditions of service, except licensed, probationary and articled teachers. They should prescribe key requirements of the process for teachers based in schools (4-10 below). LEAs should be required to take account of these requirements in the arrangements they make for the appraisal of teachers not based in schools (e.g. peripatetic staff).

6. The head teacher should decide who should appraise each teacher in a school. The Circular should specify that the appraiser should normally be the line manager of the teacher.

7. Head teachers should have two appraisers, both appointed by the chief Education Officer of the LEA. One of them must have relevant experience as a head teacher. In the case of voluntary aided, voluntary controlled and special agreement schools the appraisers should be appointed after consultation with the governing body of the school.

8. The appraisal of both teachers and head teachers should be conducted on a two year cycle, with each successive two year period treated as one appraisal programme.

9. Each appraisal programme should have the following components:

   - an initial meeting between the appraiser(s) and the teacher or head teacher being appraised (the appraisee), to clarify the purposes and to identify areas of work on which the appraisal might concentrate;
   - self appraisal by the appraisee;
   - classroom observation for teachers (on at least two occasions) and either classroom or 'task' observation (e.g. observation of the head at meetings) for head teachers;
   - review of other relevant information e.g. the work of pupils, information about duties outside the classroom;
   - an appraisal interview, providing an opportunity for genuine dialogue between the appraisee and the appraiser;
   - preparation of an appraisal statement recording the conclusions of the interview, including agreed targets for future action/professional development; and
   - a 'follow up' meeting to review progress, to be held in the second year of the programme.

10. Appraisal should be conducted against the background of sound professional criteria. Guidance on criteria should be drawn up by LEAs, in consultation with schools, taking account of the full range of national and local policies for education including the National Curriculum, publications of HMI relating to good teaching and, where appropriate, the work of teacher training institutions.

11. When collecting information for appraisal, appraisers should follow the Code of Practice set out at Appendix 4 to the report.

12. Access to appraisal statements should be restricted to the appraiser, the appraisee, the head teacher of the school and the CEO. The Circular should indicate that separate records of targets for professional development and training should be kept and that these should be made available to those planning development and training at school and LEA level. It should also indicate that proposals for action deriving from appraisal should be reported to the governing body of the school if they require an executive decision by that body or relate to the use of resources for which the governing body is responsible.

13. LEAs should be required to take account of the results of appraisals in exercising their responsibilities for staff development and training.

14. LEAs should be required to establish procedures for teachers to complain if they feel that their appraisers have acted 'unreasonably'.

15. All teachers and head teachers should be trained for appraisal, both as appraisers and as appraisees.

16. Arrangements in grant maintained schools should reflect requirements in the LEA sector as far as possible, subject to any differences flowing from their particular status.

17. LEAs and grant maintained schools should be set a target of introducing appraisal for all teachers by Summer 1994.

18. The implementation of appraisal should be closely monitored at local and national level.

19. The estimated additional teacher time required for the operation of appraisal is equivalent to 1828 FTE teachers; the cost in 1989 prices is estimated at between £36.4m and £40.5m.

Extract from the Report of the Appraisal Training Working Group
June 1986

Agreed Principles

3. Nature and purpose. The Working Group understands appraisal not as a series of perfunctory periodic events, but as a continuous and systematic process intended to help individual teachers with their professional development and career planning, and to help ensure that the in-service training and deployment of teachers matches the complementary needs of individual teachers and the schools. An appraisal system will take into account the following matters:

i) Planning the introduction of EG teachers and assessing their fitness to transfer to an MPG.

ii) Planning the participation of individual teachers in in-service training.

iii) Helping individual teachers, their head teachers and their employers to see when a new or modified assignment would help the professional development of individual teachers and improve their career prospects.

iv) Identifying the potential of teachers for career development, with an eye to their being helped by appropriate in-service training.

v) Recognition of teachers experiencing performance difficulty, the purpose being to provide help through appropriate guidance, counselling and training. Disciplinary procedures would remain quite separate, but might need to draw on relevant information from the appraisal records.

vi) Staff appointment procedures. The relevant elements of appraisal should be available to better inform those charged with the responsibility for providing references.

It will be seen that what the Working Group has in mind is a positive process, intended to raise the quality of education in schools by providing teachers with better job satisfaction, more appropriate in-service training and better planned career development based upon more informed decisions.

Issues on which comments have been requested by the Secretary of State for Education

i. To what extent should the criteria against which a teacher's work would be assessed be determined nationally?

ii. How should the results of appraisal affect the development of teachers and the management of schools; in particular:

   (a) how should appraisal inform the management of in-service training and staff development generally;

   (b) how should appraisal feed into decisions about career progression, including the award of incentive allowances; and

   (c) what should be the role of appraisal in identifying and supporting teachers who may not be performing satisfactorily, and in assisting their managers?

iii. What should be the main components of the appraisal process?

iv. What rules should be followed in the conduct of appraisal, including the selection of appraisers and arrangements for handling disagreements and disputes?

v. How should the results of appraisals be documented? Who should have access to the documents about individual teachers and/or information about the results of appraisals?

vi. On what time scale would it be appropriate to bring in Regulations requiring LEAs to introduce appraisal, and, once Regulations are in place, to require the extension of appraisal to all serving teachers, from the point of view of schools' capacity to manage the innovation alongside other work?

Bibliography

Abbott, A., (1983), 'Professional Ethics'. *American Journal of Sociology*, 88(5), 855-885.

ACAS, (1986), *Teachers' Dispute ACAS Independent Panel: Report of the Appraisal/Training Working Group* mimeo, ACAS.

Acheson, K. A. and Gall, M. D. (1987), *Techniques in the Clinical Supervision of Teachers,* (2nd Edition), Longmans: London.

Acker, S. (ed.) (1989), *Teachers, Genders and Careers*, London: Falmer Press.

Addison, B. and Al-Khalifa, E.(1988), *Sexual Harassment in Birmingham Schools and Colleges, Report of the Birmingham Teacher Survey*, 53-7, Teacher Research Group.

Al-Khalifa, E. (1989), 'Management by halves: women teachers and school management', in De Lyon, H. and Migniuolo, F. W. (eds), *Women Teachers: Issues and Experiences*, 83-96, Milton Keynes: Open University Press.

Al-Khalifa, E. (1987), 'Women's work', *Child Education*, October, 11-13.

AMMA, (1988), *Striving for Equality; multi-cultural and anti-racist education today.*

AMMA, (1985), *Women Teachers' Career Prospects.*

Austin, K. R., and Langston, D. C., (1981), 'Peer review: its impact on quality control', *Journal of Accountancy*, 152, 78-82.

Bandura, A., (1982), 'Self-efficacy mechanism in human agency', *American Psychologist*, 37(2), 122-147.

Bangar, S. and McDermott, J. (1989), 'Black women speak' in De Lyon, H. and Migniuolo, F. W. (eds), *Women Teachers: issues and experiences*, 135-153, Milton Keynes: Open University Press.

Barber, B., (1965), 'Some problems in the sociology of professions', in Lynn, K. S. (ed), *The professions in America*, Boston: Houghton-Mifflin.

Barber, L. W., (1984), *Teacher evaluation and merit pay: Background papers for the Task Force on Education for Economic Growth*, (Working paper no. TF-83-5), Denver: Education Commission of the States.

Bargh, E. (1988), 'Equal opportunities and appraisal interviewing', *AUT Woman*, No. 15, Autumn.

Bolam, R. (1984), 'Recent research on the dissemination and implementation of education innovations' in Campbell, G. (ed) *Health Education and Youth: A Review of Research and Developments*, London: Falmer Press.

Bolam, R. (1986), The National Development Centre for School Management Training in Hoyle, E., and McMahon, A., (eds), *World Yearbook of Education, 1986: The Management of Schools*, London: Kogan Page

Bolam, R., (1988), 'What is effective INSET?' in *Professional Development and INSET: Proceedings of the 1987 NFER Members' Conference*, Slough: NFER

Bollington, R. and Hopkins, D. (1987), *Teacher Appraisal for Professional Development: A Review of Research*, Cambridge Institute of Education.

Boreham, P., (1983), 'Indetermination: Professional knowledge, organization and control', *Sociological Review*, 32, 693-718.

Bradley, Howard, et al., (1988), Unpublished evaluation reports on the Appraisal Pilot Scheme Project: Cambridge Institute of Education.

Bradley, Howard, et al, (1989), *Report of the evaluation of the School Teacher Appraisal Pilot Study*, Cambridge Institute of Education, 1989

Broadfoot, P. and Osborn, M., (1988), 'What professional responsibility means to teachers: national contexts and classroom constants', *British Journal of Sociology of Education*, 9 (3)

Brook, R. H., Williams, K. N., and Avery, A. D., (1976), 'Quality assurance today and tomorrow: forecast for the future', *Annals of Internal Medicine*, 85, 809-817.

Bunnell, S. and Stephens, E. (1984), 'Teacher appraisal: a democratic approach', *School Organisation*, 4:4, 291-302.

CIE (1986) Proposal for the Evaluation of the School Teacher Appraisal Pilot Study.

Cohen, L. H., and Strauss-Zerby, S., (1984), 'Peer review of psychotherapy', American Behavioral Scientist, 27(5), 631-648.

Cunnison, S. (1989), 'Gender joking in the staffroom', in Acker, S. (ed.), *Teachers, Genders and Careers*, 151-70, London: Falmer Press.

Darling-Hammond, L., Wise, E. A. and Pease, S. R. (1983), 'Teacher evaluation in the organisational context: a review of the literature', *Review of Educational Research*, 53 (3), 285-328.

Darling-Hammond, L., (1984), 'Toledo's intern-intervention program', in Wise, A. E. et al, *Case studies for teacher evaluation: A study of effective practices*, 119-166, Santa Monica CA: The Rand Corporation.

Day, C., Whitaker, P. and Wren, D. (1987), *Appraisal and Professional Development in Primary Schools*, Milton Keynes: Open University Press.

De Lyon, H. and Migniuolo, F. W. (eds.) (1989), *Women Teachers: Issues and Experiences*, Milton Keynes: Open University Press.

DES, (1983), *Curriculum 11-16: towards a statement of entitlement: curricular reappraisal in action*, DES, HMSO (distributor)

DES and Welsh Office, (1983), *Teaching Quality*, Cmnd 8836, HMSO.

DES and Welsh Office, (1985), *Better Schools*, Cmnd 9469, HMSO.

DES, (1985), *Quality in Schools: evaluation and appraisal*, HMSO.

DES, (1987), *School Teachers' Pay and Conditions Document*, HMSO.

DES, (1988), *The New Teacher in School: a Survey by H. M. Inspectors in England and Wales, 1987*, London: HMSO.

DES, (1989), *Developments in the Appraisal of Teachers*, A Report by HM Inspectorate, DES.

DES (1989), *Records of achievement: Report of the Records of Achievement National Steering Committee*, January.

DES, (1989), *School teacher appraisal: a national framework,* Report of the National Steering Group on the School Teacher Appraisal Pilot Study, HMSO.

Equal Opportunities Commission, (1985), *Code of Practice: Equal Opportunity Policies Procedures and Practices in Employment,* HMSO.

Equal Opportunities Commission (1985), *Equal Opportunities and the Woman Teacher: Guidelines for the elimination of sex and marriage discrimination and the promotion of equality of opportunity in teacher employment,* EOC.

Flores, A. and Johnson, D. G., (1983), 'Collective responsibility and professional roles', *Ethics,* 93, 537-545.

Freidson, E., (1970), *The Profession of Medicine,* New York: Dodd, Mead.

Friedson, E., (1973), 'Professionalization and the organization of middle class labour in post-industrial society', in Halmas, P. (ed), *Professionalization and social change,* (Sociological Review Monograph 20), Keele: University of Keele.

Freidson, E., (1983), 'The theory of the professions: the state of the art' in Dingwall, R., and Lewis, P., (eds), *The Sociology of the Professions: Lawyers, Doctors and Others,* London: Macmillan.

Fullan, M., (1982), *The Meaning of Educational Change,* Toronto: OISE Press.

Galton, M., Simon, B. and Croll, P., (1980), *Inside the primary classroom,* London: Routledge and Kegan Paul, 1980

Gilligan, C. (1982), *In a Different Voice; psychological theory and women's development,* Cambridge, Mass.: Harvard University Press.

Grace, G., (1978), *Teachers, Ideology and Control: a Study of Urban Education,* London: Routledge and Kegan Paul

Halmos, P., (ed), (1973), *Professionalization and Social Change: Sociological Review Monograph No. 20,* Keele: University of Keele.

Hewton, Eric (1988), *The Appraisal Interview: An Approach to Training For Teachers and School Management,* Milton Keynes: Open University Press.

Holly, P., and Southworth, C., (1989), *The Developing School*, London: Falmer.

Hopkins, D., (ed), (1986), *In-service Training and Educational Development*, London: Croom Helm.

Hoyle, E., (1980), 'Professionalisation and de-professionalisation in education' in Hoyle, E., and Megarry, J., (eds), *World Yearbook of Education, 1980: the Professional Development of Teachers*, London: Kogan Page.

Hoyle, E., (1988), 'Teachers' roles and careers' in *Managing Schools*, E325, Block 4, Milton Keynes: Open University Press.

Hoyle, E., (1982), 'The professionalisation of teachers: a paradox', *British Journal of Educational Studies*, 30 (2).

Hughes, M., (1980), 'Reconciling professional and administrative concerns' in Bush, T., et al, (eds), *Approaches to School Management*, London: Harper and Row/O.U. Press.

Hunt, K., (1982), 'Are they taking the peer out of peer review?', *Medical Economics*, 20, 183-187.

ILEA, (1984), *Improving Secondary Schools: report of the Committee on Curriculum and organisation of secondary schools*, chaired by Dr David H. Hargreaves ILEA, 1984.

ILEA, (1985), *Improving Primary Schools: report of the Committee on Primary Education*, chaired by Norman Thomas, ILEA, 1985.

ILEA, (1987), 'Black and ethnic minority teachers' own account of their experience', in ILEA Education Committee, *Policy Sub-Committee Equal Opportunities Section Report*, 13 July.

Jackson, P., (1968), *Life in Classrooms*, New York: Holt, Rinehart, Winston.

James, C. R. and Newman, J. C. (1985), 'Staff appraisal schemes in comprehensive schools: a regional survey of current practice in the South Midlands and the South West of England', *Educational Management and Administration*, 13(3).

James, G. (1988), *Performance Appraisal*, ACAS Work Research Unit.

Joint Commission on Accreditation of Hospitals, (1982), *Accreditation Manual for Hospitals 1982*, Chicago: JCAH.

Joyce, B. and Showers, B. (1980), 'Improving in-service training; the messages of research', *Education and Leadership*, 37 (5), pp. 379-85.

Larson, M., (1977), *The Rise of Professionalism*, Berkeley: University of California Press.

Lipsky, M., (1980), *Street-level Bureaucracy*, New York: Russell Sage.

Lohr, K. N., Winkler, J. D. and Brook, R. H., (1981), *Peer Review and Technology Assessment in Medicine*, Santa Monica CA: Rand Corporation.

Lohr, K. N., and Brook, R. H., (1984), *Quality assurance in medicine*, Santa Monica CA: Rand Corporation.

Lyons, G. and Stenning, R. (1986), *Managing Staff in Schools: A Handbook*, London: Hutchinson.

Mackenzie, D. E., (1983), 'Research for school improvement: An appraisal of some recent trends', *Educational Researcher*, 12, 5-17.

Manning, P. R., (1982), 'Continuing education and quality assurance', in Selbmann, H. K., and Uberla, K. K. (eds), *Quality Assessment of Medical Care*, 175-180, Gerlingen: Bleicher Verlag.

Manzer, R. A., (1970), *Teachers and Politics*, Manchester: Manchester University Press

McGreal, Thomas L., (1983), *Successful Teacher Evaluation*, ASCD, Alexandra, Va.

McKellar, B. (1989), 'Only the fittest will survive: black women and education' in Acker, S. (ed.), *Teachers, Genders and Careers*, 69-85, London: Falmer Press.

McLaughlin, M. L., and Pfeifer, R. S., (1988), *Teacher Evaluation*, Teachers College Press

McMahon, A. (ed) (1987), *Consortium of Teacher Appraisal Pilot Schemes: Report on the First National Conference for LEA Co-ordinators, May 5/6th 1987*, National Development Centre for School Management Training, Bristol University, School of Education.

McMillan, J., (1974), 'Peer review and professional standards for psychologists rendering personal health services', *Professional Psychology*, 5, 51-58.

Mortimore, Peter, et al, (1988), *School Matters: the junior years*, Open Books.

National Development Centre for School Management Training (1989), *Consortium of School Teacher Appraisal Pilot Schemes, Eighth National Conference for LEA Co-ordinators 22nd-24th May 1989*.

Nelson, E. A., Vanwagener, R. K. and Brook, W. C. (1987), 'Factors affecting the reliability and stability of Teacher Performance Ratings', Paper prepared for meeting of the American Educational Research Association, Arizona State University, mimeo.

Newcastle-upon-Tyne LEA, (1987), *STAFF (School Teacher Appraisal Formative Framework) Manual and Action Plan*, Newcastle-upon-Tyne Appraisal Project.

Newcastle-upon-Tyne LEA, (1988), *Headteacher Appraisal - a position paper*, unpublished.

Nias, J., (1989), *Primary Teachers Talking: a Study of Teaching as Work*, London: Routledge.

Niblett, B. (1986), *Appraisal: NDC Resource Bank Annotated Bibliography No. 1*, 2nd edition, NDC.

Niblett, B. (1988), *Appraisal: Supplement to Annotated Bibliography No. 1*, 2nd edition, NDC.

Peterson, K. and Kauchak, D., (1982), *Teacher Evaluation: Perspectives, Practices, and Promises*, Salt Lake City: University of Utah.

Peterson, P. L., (1979), 'Direct instruction reconsidered', in Peterson, P. L. and Walberg, H. J. (eds), *Research on teaching*, Berkeley CA: McCutchan.

Pratzner, F. C., (1984), 'Quality of school life: foundations for improvement', *Educational Researcher*, 13(3), 20-25.

Ranger, C. (1988), *Ethnic Minority School Teachers: a survey of eight Local Education Authorities*, Commission for Racial Equality.

Rhodes, C. D. M. (1988), 'Practical appraisal in primary schools' in Bell, L. (ed.), *Appraising Teachers in Schools; a practical guide*, 44-57, Routledge.

Ridyard, Keith (1989), *Appraisal with the Human Touch*, AMMA Report.

Rosenshine, B. V., (1979), 'Content, time and direct instruction', in Peterson, P. L. and Walberg, H. J. (eds), *Research on teaching*, Berkeley CA: McCutchan.

Rothstein, W. G., (1969), 'Engineers and the functionalist model of the professions', in Perucci, R., and Gerstl, J. E., (eds), *Engineers and the social system*, 73-98, New York: Wiley.

Rueschmeyer, D., (1983), 'Professional autonomy and the social context of expertise' in Dingwall and Lewis, *op cit*.

Rutter, Michael, *et al*, (1979), *Fifteen Thousand Hours: secondary schools and their effects on children*, London: Open Books, 1979

Sechrest, L., and Hoffman, P. E., (1982), 'The philosophical underpinnings of peer review', *Professional Psychology*, 13(1), 14-18.

Shakeshaft, C. (1989), Unpublished paper given to the American Educational Research Association, April.

Shavelson, R. J., and Dempsey-Attwood, N., (1976), 'Generalizability of measures of teacher bahavior', *Review of Educational Research*, 46, 553-612.

Soar, R. S., (1972), *Follow Through Classroom Process Measurement and Pupil Growth*, Gainesville: University of Florida.

Somerset LEA, (1988), *Head Light - A Handbook of information for Headteachers in Somerset LEA's Review and Development Pilot Project*, unpublished.

Spender, D. (1985), *Man Made Language*, 2nd edition, 41-51 and 120-125, London: Routledge and Kegan Paul.

Spender, D. (1989), *Invisible Women: the schooling scandal*, 56-68, London: Women's Press.

Stacey, D. C., Kuligowski, B. and Holdzkom, D. (1988), 'Evaluation of the effectiveness of the North Carolina Teacher Performance Appraisal System', North Carolina: Department of Public Instruction, mimeo.

Stillman, A. and Grant, M. (1989), *The LEA Adviser; a changing role*, 52-56, NFER/Nelson.

Stodolsky, S., (1984), 'Teacher evaluation: the limits of looking', *Educational Researcher*, 13, 11-22.

Suffolk LEA, (1985), *Those Having Torches ... Teacher Appraisal: A Study*, Suffolk LEA.

Suffolk LEA, (1987), *In the Light of Torches: Teacher Appraisal: A Further Study*, The Industrial Society.

Suffolk LEA, (1989), *On from Torches: an account of a Suffolk private scheme*, prepared by the County Appraisal Team, Suffolk LEA.

Sykes, G., (1984), *The Conference* (mimeograph), Stanford CA: Stanford University.

Theaman, M., (1984), 'The impact of peer review on professional practice', *American Psychologist*, 37, 406-414.

Tomlinson, J. R. G., (1980), *Reflections on Curriculum Development*, University College of Swansea, 1980.

Trethowan, David (1987), *Appraisal and Target Setting*, London: Harper and Row.

Turner, G. and Clift, P. (1985), *A First Review and Register of School and College-based Teacher Appraisal Schemes*, Milton Keynes: Open University Press.

Turner, G., Nuttall, D. and Clift, P. (1986), 'Staff Appraisal', in Hoyle, E. and McMahon, A. (eds), *World Yearbook of Education 1986: The Management of Schools*, London: Kogan Page.

Turner, G. and Clift, P. (1987), *A Second Review and Register of School and College-based Teacher Appraisal Schemes*, Milton Keynes: Open University Press.

Walsh, K., (1987), 'The politics of teacher appraisal' in Lawn, M., and Grace, G., *Teachers: the Culture and Politics of Work*, London: Falmer Press.

Wise, A. E., Darling-Hammond, L., McLaughlin, M. W. and Bernstein, H. T. (1984), *Teacher Evaluation: A Study of Effective Practices*, Santa Monica, CA: The Rand Corporation.

Index

The Contributors

Ray Bolam is Director of the National Development Centre for School Management Training, University of Bristol, which was appointed to co-ordinate the appraisal pilot studies.

Howard Bradley is Director of the Cambridge Institute of Education and was appointed as national evaluator of the appraisal pilot studies.

Terry Buckler is a headteacher and Divisional Secretary of the National Union of Teachers in Cumbria. He has been on the Appraisal Steering Group in Cumbria since inception.

Linda Darling-Hammond was Director of the Education and Human Resources Program at the Rand Corporation and is now Professor of Education at Teachers College, Columbia University.

Alan Evans is a Research Consultant at the School of Education, University of Wales College of Cardiff, and was the Vice Chair of the National Steering Group on appraisal of schoolteachers.

Victor L. Gane is a former headteacher and was the co-ordinator of the appraisal pilot study in Somerset.

Eric Hoyle is Professor of Education at the University of Bristol School of Education.

Agnes McMahon is Research Fellow at the NDCSMT, University of Bristol, and has been responsible for the co-ordination of the appraisal pilot studies.

Barbara Payne is a secondary headteacher in Newcastle-upon-Tyne, whose school was involved in the pilot study.

Andy Smith is an education and training consultant who has worked on appraisal training with several of the pilot study authorities. He is involved in the development of appraisal in 20 local authorities.

Meryl Thompson is a senior assistant secretary at the Assistant Masters and Mistresses Association and represented AMMA on the NSG.

John Tomlinson is Professor of Education and Director of the Institute of Education at the University of Warwick and was formerly Chief Education Officer in Cheshire.

Maeve Willis is a former headteacher who was appointed to co-ordinate the appraisal pilot study in Croydon.